Three Prayers You'll Want to Pray

GEORGE H. DONIGIAN

 Morehouse Publishing
NEW YORK

Morehouse Publishing, 4785 Linglestown Road, Suite 101, Harrisburg, PA 17112

Morehouse Publishing, 19 East 34th Street, New York, NY 10016

Morehouse Publishing is an imprint of Church Publishing Incorporated.

www.churchpublishing.org

Cover design by Laurie Klein Westhafer
Typeset by Denise Hoff

Library of Congress Cataloging-in-Publication Data

Donigian, George Hovaness.
      Three prayers you'll want to pray / George H. Donigian.
         pages cm
      Includes bibliographical references.
      ISBN 978-0-8192-2906-9 (pbk.)—ISBN 978-0-8192-2907-6 (ebook)
1. Prayer—Christianity.   2. Prayers.   I. Title.
BV210.3.D66 2014
242'.8—dc23
                                                              2014022188

Printed in the United States of America

For the Six:
Elizabeth Donigian, Caitlin Stokes,
Robert Donigian, Sara Unrue, Rebecca
Unrue, George Donigian, Jr.
and all their loves
and all our conversations

CONTENTS

EPIGRAPH

"In the time of your life, live—so that in that good time there shall be no ugliness or death for yourself or for any life your life touches. Seek goodness everywhere, and when it is found, bring it out of its hiding place and let it be free and unashamed. . . .

In the time of your life, live—so that in that wondrous time you shall not add to the misery and sorrow of the world, but shall smile to the infinite delight and mystery of it."

—William Saroyan
(from Credo in *The Time of Your Life*)

THREE PRAYERS YOU'LL WANT TO PRAY: AN INTRODUCTION

Why would you want to pray these three particular prayers? Did I pull them at random from the *Gigantic Book of Prayers, Meditations, and Related Items*? No—and that book has not been published.

Here are some of the reasons I chose these three prayers. I like them. I love them. They challenge me. They give me a sense of hope. They speak of God's unconditional love and of my own responsibility in the world. They direct me to works of justice and mercy. One of the prayers grounds me in a history of God's liberation and points me to the unfolding future of God's love. Another of these prayers reminds me in very pointed ways that I am not in charge of the universe and that I have responsibility to know myself, especially what motivates me, better. The third prayer connects me with people around the world and throughout history. So I pray them. Some days the words flow. Other days the words struggle to have voice. I am no expert in prayer. I would not trust anyone who claimed to be an expert in prayer because such a claim is arrogant and the opposite of prayer. I am an ordinary person who tries to live with an awareness of God's unconditional love for all people, and I pray in that spirit.

The first prayer comes from a diplomat. The second prayer comes from a theologian. The third prayer comes from a rabbi. Stick with those identifications for a bit. Any other identification begins to load a little baggage onto this introduction.

A diplomat, a theologian, and a rabbi—that sounds like the beginning of a joke. Maybe they walk into a bar or they meet at the Orange Diamond Casino or they are on a faltering airplane with only two parachutes remaining among the three. Many people carry stereotypes of rabbis, theologians, and diplomats. Perhaps the most common stereotype is that of the diplomat in cutaway jacket and striped pants at a formal reception. Or that of a black homburg-wearing rabbi who asks questions in response to other questions. We may imagine theologians in their ivory towers, out of touch with the everyday.

I'd like to consider what a rabbi, a theologian, and a diplomat might have in common, especially their common best attributes. They have principles, and they take positions based on those principles. They understand a higher purpose in life or perhaps we may call it a deeper purpose in life. They respect other people. They affirm that other people also have a deeper purpose in life. Rabbi, theologian, diplomat: at their best they evoke our best and our deeper purpose. When that happens, these three show us new dimensions of life, new directions and perspectives.

Rabbi, theologian, and diplomat: they do not defend the old way of living, but point us to an unfolding revelation of divine intent for the world. They speak of the departure of the old order and the coming of the new. Rabbi, theologian, and diplomat demonstrate wisdom attributed to multiple sources: when faced with two choices, choose the third option.

When I think of rabbi, theologian, and diplomat, I also think that one attribute the three persons share is that they hold much information in confidence. They do not keep secrets for the sake of blackmail or for the sake of gossip. Rather, the stories and information they know become part of the solution to questions and problems they face later. When we read and use these prayers, we will first see language that seems general; the more often each prayer is read or prayed, however, the more specific those concepts become and the more they connect with the life of the one who is praying. Rabbi, theologian, and diplomat use a language of confidentiality that helps reveal.

My Perspective

Let me make some connections between my story and the subject of prayer. In some ways, the whole of this little book works as an introduction, but I want you to learn a little about what I think relevant from my life story to this book. I am an Armenian-American or a person of Armenian descent. My family came to the United States to escape the genocide of Armenian people in the Ottoman Empire. When 1915 began, about two million Armenians lived in the Ottoman Empire (sometimes called the Turkish Empire). The genocide began with events on April 24, and by the end of the genocidal period, approximately 1.25 million Armenians were dead. Why? Ottoman leadership wanted to maintain the control and power it held throughout the nineteenth century while early twentieth-century geopolitical realities were changing the dynamics of that power. Armenians, a Christian minority within the empire, became a convenient target. The rhetoric of 1915 sounds much like the later rhetoric of Adolf Hitler in the 1930s concerning Jews in Germany. Many of the Armenians who survived and stayed in what became modern Turkey changed their surnames to blend more effectively into that place. Other survivors escaped and began to create new lives. Genocide is not only about killing people, but it attempts a total annihilation of any signs of that group of people. Armenian cemeteries were destroyed, and Armenian churches became mosques or jails.

My father's father rolled his extra shirt, a coffee pot, and two gold coins in a small prayer rug to make his journey. My mother's father tried to come to the United States, was turned away because of his age, and ended up in Brazil. He came to the United States a few years later. Given what I know of my grandparents, I suspect that they all would have preferred stable lives in the Old Country to being uprooted in adulthood and tossed into the upheaval of learning a new language and different cultural survival skills. My parents tried to hide the facts of the genocide from my brother and me, a common survivor syndrome response. Even though we did not learn directly about the genocide, we could not forget it. As a boy growing up among survivors who tried not to speak of the horror of the genocide, I read some of the literature written by Armenians in the United States and realized that the impact of the genocide was central to much of that writing. When I went with my family to Armenian Church cultural festivals, I became aware that the church depended upon people to donate funds in memory of various relatives killed by the Turks. While my parents could not speak directly of the genocide, I learned that my father had two brothers under the age of ten who were killed in the genocide and that my mother's family also suffered losses. Later I learned more of the impact of the genocide and its aftermath on my family, including involvement in a plot to kill an Armenian archbishop who spoke of the need for forgiveness of the Turks.

One of my first lessons in prayer was an Armenian blessing before meals, which loosely translated begins, "Whatever we eat, whatever we drink, we give you thanks." To those who escaped by night through mountains and sheep pastures, past the patrols of Turkish gendarmes, and who came without documentation through Syria and Lebanon, who settled in France and who crossed the Atlantic to Ellis Island, "whatever we eat, whatever we drink" carries far different nuances than our contemporary use of "whatever."

Beyond the reference point of Armenian experience, *place* is significant in forming a basis for my prayer. I grew up in a small and somewhat unusual town in Virginia; the population included Armenians, Chinese, Greeks, Japanese, Lebanese, Syrians, and Turks. I attended public schools there and also went to Fork Union Military Academy as a 13-year-old in the ninth grade. Connected to the Virginia Baptist Assembly, Fork Union had chapel six days a week and inspections every day. I learned to shave, but my daily beard shadow never seemed to pass inspection so I vowed to grow a beard when I left that school. I learned to march and to do the basics of the manual of arms. I learned many military rules and regulations. As did many others who went to such heavily regimented schools, I also learned a variety of ways to evade those regulations and rules.

None of us escape the importance of work and vocation. I am ordained in the United Methodist Church. I have worked or served as a pastor of several relatively small congregations. I moved into religious publishing and was a developer of curriculum resources for churches, an editor, a marketing person, and a publisher. Before I did those things, I grew up in the family grocery store where I learned some butcher skills and more.

I've been unemployed. I've known the bitterness of losing a highly anticipated promotion and the grief of losing a job. I've experienced the disappointment of seeing the wrong people promoted and also seeing corporate entities fire people who spoke necessary truth to the organization. I've experienced satisfaction in work done well.

Music and Prayer

Before I experienced the world of work or any of the other areas of life that are intended to prepare us for adulthood, I fell in love with music. By the time I was three, I wanted to play the piano, something that scared my father. I loved the exuberant music of Ludwig van Beethoven and Aram Khachaturian even before I knew who these composers were. I loved the music of bands at Armenian cultural festivals and the sacred music of church. When I was a little older, my parents tired of hearing my renditions of "Come On-A My House." Many years later I learned that this favorite song was written by two Armenian cousins: Ross Bagdasarian, more well known as Dave Seville, who created The Chipmunks, and William Saroyan, a Pulitzer Prize winner. Eventually a beat-up multiple-owner piano arrived in our house. I discovered that it had been a player piano, but no music rolls came with it. That piano served well for two years until my mother decided that I was "serious" about music and bought another second-hand piano. (Built in June 1936, that second piano lived to the age of 74 when the cracked soundboard and other problems called for full retirement.) Later came an alto saxophone. Still in childhood, I began to play the organ at church services and then went through a period of playing rock organ on Saturday nights and sacred music on Sunday mornings.

I connect music and prayer, and I hope that you will see this connection as it grows throughout the book. When we begin to learn to play a musical instrument, we learn scales. A musical scale is simply a set of notes ordered by set frequencies. In Western music, scales generally consist of seven notes that either ascend or descend. When you sang or listened to the Christmas carol "Deck the Halls," you may not have realized that the opening phrase begins with a simple descending scale. Take time to hum the opening line and notice the descent and ascent: "Deck the halls with boughs of holly." We are singing part of a scale. Think of a scale as a basic foundation for music practice and performance. Musicians practice scales throughout their lifetimes because these scales continue to develop technique, touch, tone, and more. We practice scales until the fingering of the notes becomes as natural as breathing.

Scales are best practiced when no one else is listening. We play scales over and over and over again. As we practice and learn these scales, we make mistakes. Our fingers go to the wrong notes. If we are playing scales on the piano, one hand may go faster than the other hand. We practice, and we practice more. Our fingers gain a certain memory of how to play an

A Major scale and what makes playing that scale different from another scale. We practice over and over and over again so that the brain–muscle connection understands the different techniques. Scales are basic and necessary for learning to play music, but audiences do not generally listen to the playing of scales. The best place to practice scales is in a relatively soundproof room where no one else can audit the practice.

From the practice of instrumental technique through scales and other exercises, we begin to play music in small groups or ensembles. I consider a musical ensemble as a group of two to eleven musicians. (With twelve or more musicians, the interpersonal and musical dynamics of the group change.) Imagine such a group in a variety of settings and with different instrumental combinations. You may see a rock trio with two electric guitarists and a drummer. A classical quartet with viola, violin, cello, and piano may appear to your mind's eye. You may envision the jazz quintet that I see: saxophone, trumpet, bass, drums, and keyboard. No matter the type of music, musicians in such an ensemble are in conversation with one another. No one stands before them to give them direction. They base their playing on a common consent, and when such a group does not agree on basics of time and tune, then the music sounds terrible.

Ensemble playing is much more fun than sitting inside a practice room or closet or even on a dock while practicing scales. When we play music with a small group, we listen to and depend on others while we also strive to do our best work. In such small-group play, we stand alone as solitary instrumentalists gathered with other solitary instrumentalists, and we become very much aware that our combined efforts will long exceed our solitary gifts.

After playing music in small groups, we may move on to play in larger bands or orchestras. The large band has a personality that differs from that of an ensemble. Such a large musical group plays broader categories of music and is capable of many different sounds. The musical instrumentation, tones, and dynamics are different. Leadership becomes more important than with an ensemble or in the scale closet. Whereas one person played saxophone in that jazz ensemble, the large band may have eight saxophone players. Whereas one person played violin in the quartet, sixteen violinists may play in an orchestra. Our individual voices or instruments are not as important as the magnitude of this multi-level orchestral sound.

Some prayers are like scales and best prayed in solitude and far from interruption. The diplomat's prayer falls into this category. We can slow our breathing as we pray these words and let this prayer grow in silent solitude.

Other prayers belong to small groups. The theologian's prayer is a primary example of the group or ensemble prayer. We may pray it by ourselves, but the prayer grows deeper when we unite in a small group that prays this prayer as one voice. The rabbi's prayer evokes the orchestral approach to prayer. Individuals know the lines, but we pray it best when we are together with a large group of people and when we recognize that we pray this prayer with people scattered around the world and throughout time.

Forming New Traditions

We pray in our contemporary culture in many different ways, perhaps failing to understand the breadth of that diversity. Twitter, Instagram, Pinterest, Facebook, and other social networks offer us opportunities to communicate the variety of our senses of gratitude, outrage, thanksgiving, anger, wonder, grief, injustice, love, dismay, and woe. Tweets and posts and photos describe our moods, share our feelings, and establish conversational pathways about birth and death and all activities between the two poles of life on earth. And you ask, *So what does this have to do with a book on prayer?*

Through social networks we have opportunity to express our emotional and physical and mental states. We tell our stories. We give expression to our inner lives and to our outer circumstances. We keep track of our lives as if we were keeping a more formal diary or journal. What we communicate is shared with those who have been part of our lives for years and to those we know only in their online identities. In a similar way, prayer offers us opportunity to connect with God and to be as honestly transparent with God as we are with the variety of friends and other connections in digital space.

We are praying. Our prayers may not fit the model of prayer that some people would require. After all, some people teach that prayer must follow an ACTS (Adoration, Confession, Thanksgiving, Supplication) or a "five-finger method" or some other device. Other people teach that only if certain words are used will God hear a prayer. Those claims are misleading and perhaps misguided. I believe that God invites us to the dance of prayer. The words and forms that we use matter very little compared to the attitude and expectation that we bring.

Those people who would teach specific models of prayer are holding onto a tradition they received. Is the tradition right? More important, what is tradition? Our creative daily actions continually form new traditions. Whether the new tradition concerns a sports event or a special date on the calendar, our traditions remind us of past–present–future time. Whenever we celebrate an annual special event or day, tradition connects us with earlier years and nudges us to anticipate future celebrations. We gather for our personal traditions, enjoying them and the friends who become part of the festivity. We participate in activities that are specific to the day or moment. We take pleasure in special foods or games or other aspects of the tradition. We create ritual practices for our traditions (such as how to set up the chairs for the homecoming tailgate event or who is the undisputed authority for the game always played at the gathering), and we understand their significance. What do we do then with the traditions we inherit from others? What if we have inherited the practice without the history of its significance? Do we abandon those traditions, reinvent them, give them new meanings, discover that the old meaning makes sense, or replace these traditions with something entirely different? Every one of us will offer a different response, and the answer will vary within us over time.

Tradition is an odd word that has come to carry some political baggage. Many people read or hear the words "we believe in the traditional faith" or "traditional family values" and begin to cringe. I know that I do. I want to ask, "How do you define 'traditional faith'? Whose tradition? Does that tradition go back to the third century or does it go back to 1958?" I want to dive into our understanding of tradition because many times people use the word *tradition* when they actually mean custom or conventional wisdom. In *No Man Is an Island*, Thomas Merton described tradition as life-giving and fertile, whereas custom, he declared, was sterile and stagnant. Convention is simply a casual acceptance of statements without seeking any validation. Convention or custom births the statements of opinion that my father would make, which usually began "They tell me that . . . ." "Who is *they*?"

I would ask him, not in hostility but to learn. Because he did not know who they were, my father would usually shake his head in disgust and walk away from the conversation. Convention thus is simply accepted without question. Tradition comes alive because we question its meaning and purpose. As we ask questions of purpose, we wrestle intellectually with those concepts. We begin to experience the significance of those traditions, and they give birth to innovation and freshness within our lives. Tradition is creative, whereas convention simply expects us to remain the same. Conventional wisdom teaches us to go along and thus get along with others. Conventional wisdom tends to breed fear and anxiety because we see matters that are unjust and yet are expected to avoid asking questions. Tradition leads us to the wisdom to say that the emperor is naked and abusing power. At its best, tradition nourishes us, giving us deep roots and empowering us to contribute to the growth of tradition. Convention encourages us to do nothing and try to remain the same. I do not care for convention for the sake of convention; I value tradition, and so the three prayers that you'll want to pray with me are rooted in tradition, but their approach to God and to our lives is always fresh and always becoming new. The three prayers of this book are grounded in tradition, but they are not traditional and they should not fall into the category of conventional wisdom. If they are considered custom or convention, I think their originators would be upset.

I pray that you will find these three prayers of tremendous depth and value and that you will grow to love them, that you will practice them, and that you will live the reality that they point toward.

Prayer

1

Scale: The Diplomat's Prayer

During a medical exam in the emergency room, the doctor asked me, "What do you do?" His earlier questions attempted to learn why I had fallen for the third time in a month. On this fall my nose broke when I hit concrete steps. The CT scan showed only a broken nose. The doctor eliminated stroke and TMI as potential causes for the falls. My heart was beating well and did not indicate a heart attack. I felt fine, but I was in the hospital for the second time in a month and for the fourth time in two years while different medical teams tried to penetrate the mysterious cause of my sudden downward drops.

"I write and edit books and pastor a small church. It's a part-time position—whatever 'part-time' means for a pastor."

"What do you write?"

"I'm currently writing a book on prayers you'll want to pray. One of the prayers comes from a man named Dag Hammarskjold, and it goes like this: 'For all that has been—Thanks! / To all that shall be—Yes!'"

"I like that," said the doctor. "I'm a Jain, and that prayer covers a lot of territory. Repeat it so I can learn to pray it myself."

For all that has been—Thanks!

To all that shall be—Yes!

Dag Hammarskjold wrote those two lines in *Markings*, a journal he prepared for posthumous publication. The words may not seem like a typical prayer, which usually includes a salutation (God, or Eternal God, or Holy One, or any of the infinite titles we prefer to identify the Ultimate One). Most prayers include conclusions, but this prayer remains marvelously open ended. To me, Hammarskjold's two simple lines embrace all the fullness and complexity of our lives. Take time now to read aloud the two lines of the prayer. Let those two lines rest in your head and your heart, your sense of being.

I do not always agree with the notion of thanksgiving for all that has happened, especially not in the moment. When I was twenty-one years old, I gave a deposition in the legal action that my mother brought to declare my father no longer mentally competent to operate his business interests. I explained in that deposition what I knew concerning the family grocery store and rental properties. Two years earlier I left college to operate the grocery store during one of my father's hospitalizations. Giving the deposition created anguish and other emotional turmoil for me, compounded seven months later when my father died. Looking back, I realize that his diabetes and heart problems contributed to his business problems. For all that has been—Thanks? That lesson I would have preferred not to experience! Not for that chaos felt in my life and in the lives of countless children caught in the triangulation of their parents' battles. On the other hand, I learned enough to avoid the same mistakes with my own family.

The Diplomat

Dag Hammarskjold's life is relatively easy to outline, but in other ways Hammarskjold's life is as unknown to us as the lives of the mystics who influenced him.

Born in 1905 to an influential Swedish family, Hammarskjold earned multiple degrees, including law and finance, and first worked for the Central Bank of Sweden. Hammarskjold felt a calling to civic or government service and followed the example of his father, who was Sweden's Prime Minister from 1914 until 1917, and other relatives, who had served the Swedish government as far back as the seventeenth century. In 1949 Hammarskjold became a Cabinet Secretary in the Swedish government. In 1953 he became the second Secretary General of the relatively new United Nations. He organized the machinery of the new institution, born after World War II in the hope that dialogue could stop the launch of war. The United Nations Assembly reelected him in 1957. On September 18, 1961, Hammarskjold was flying to negotiate a peace treaty in the Congo when the airplane crashed and the 16 people on board died. Conspiracy theories abound concerning the plane crash and whether Hammarskjold's death resulted from Cold War maneuvers between the superpowers. No matter the cause, Hammarskjold's death was tragic. He may have been able to negotiate a lasting peace settlement in the Congo and saved the lives of many. (In the FWIW department: Barbara Kingsolver powerfully and poignantly described the civil war in Congo in *The Poisonwood Bible*, and I recommend her novel as another way to understand the situation to which Hammarskjold tried to bring peace.)

Friends found a manuscript and an undated letter in Hammarskjold's apartment after his death. The letter addressed the Swedish Under-Secretary for Foreign Affairs and described Hammarskjold's private diary. Hammarskjold collected different portions of his diary in the manuscript to become "the only true 'profile' that can be drawn." He concluded the letter:

> If you find them worth publishing, you have my permission to do so—as a sort of white book concerning my negotiations with myself—and with God. (*Markings*, p. v)

That manuscript became the book titled *Markings*.

The manuscript begins with this quotation from Meister Eckhart: "Only the hand that erases can write the true thing." The published journal ranges from 1925 until 1961. The entries are not divided evenly among these years. Hammarskjold offers only a few entries from 1925–1930 and then jumps to 1941–1942 followed by 1945–1949. After these groupings, Hammarskjold offers single-year clusters of reflection. Did he follow the wisdom of Meister Eckhart and erase material? Absolutely, and in the material that remains we begin to glimpse truth.

In his Foreword to *Markings*, the poet W. H. Auden described Hammarskjold's reflections as an effort "to unite in one life the *via activa* and the *via contempla tiva*" (*Markings*, p. xx). We see Hammarskjold the diplomat in the most public platform, visible and known across the globe. His actions ranged from the ordinary routine of building the then-novel global enterprise called the United Nations to negotiating the 1955 release of Korean War prisoners in China to the 1957 intervention in the Suez Crisis between Egypt and Israel, Britain, and France. During the Cold War period between the United States and the Soviet Union, both nations criticized Hammarskjold for seeming to prefer the other nation. He worked for peace. While he used his gifts and abilities for the cause of peace, he practiced a quiet diplomacy and did not seek celebrity status. From *Markings* we get a sense that his quiet diplomacy grew from his quiet practice of prayer and contemplation.

In a radio program called *This I Believe*, Hammarskjold offered this autobiographical assessment:

> From generations of soldiers and government officials on my father's side I inherited a belief that no life was more satisfactory than one of selfless service to your country—or humanity. . . . From scholars and clergymen on my mother's side I inherited a belief that, in the very radical sense of the Gospels, all . . . were equals as children of God, and should be met and treated by us as our masters in God. (*This I Believe*, 1953)

Hammarskjold's life seems marked by a purpose that went beyond the day-to-day experience most of us have. His vocational calling remains a rare model of heroism.

The Mystical Inner Life

From the visible external markers of Hammarskjold's life, we begin to see the inner convictions that shaped his diplomatic efforts. That leads to the second question of biographical inquiry: Who or what beyond family influenced Hammarskjold's spirituality? Based on his writings and conversations, spiritual direction came from the writings of some medieval spiritual guides. In addition to Meister Eckhart, Hammarskjold grew familiar with Julian of

Norwich, "The Cloud of Unknowing," and St. John of the Cross. All practiced and taught the importance of contemplation. Perhaps the most well known of the contemplative moments came in the vision of Julian of Norwich, who lived from 1342 to 1416. As with Hammarskjold and other mystics, we know little about Julian. She described herself as ignorant, but she could write—quite an accomplishment for a woman of that time in England! Julian received a vision of a hazelnut, and in that vision she realized three things: 1) God made it, 2) God loves it, and 3) God keeps and preserves it. After another contemplative experience, Julian wrote, "but all shall be well, and all shall be well, and all manner of thing shall be well." Her statement seems harmless and somewhat ordinary until we realize that Bubonic Plague devastated the population of England and much of the world in the fourteenth century. Fear of the disease gripped many people. Those who heard or read Julian's message received good news.

The mystics who influenced Hammarskjold taught a contemplative means of prayer. Meister Eckhart (1260–1327) wrote that the best way to enter spiritual life is by keeping silent and letting God work and speak. John of the Cross and other mystics taught that our best prayers use no words, but are responses to God's invitation to be still and to know God's love. The mystic way invites us to journey spiritually not with our intellects, but our hearts.

The Certain Past

I repeat the two lines of Hammarskjold's prayer often in this chapter and in life.

> For all that has been—Thanks!
> To all that shall be—Yes!

These two simple lines evoke a sense of wonder and gratitude, and they serve to remind me of tests and temptations endured and yet to come. Hammarskjold's prayer reminds me of the good that comes in even the worst of times as we and others respond to the mysteries of disease and suffering.

Some moments do not generate gratitude. Some portions of life seem devoid of thanksgiving, and yet we may discover gratitude when we look back at these harsh times. Human beings remain free to choose. We choose evil or good. We act, knowing that we cannot foresee the consequences of our actions. Some actions, done with good intentions, end with negative results. Other actions, which seem harmful, lead to positive results. God does not pull strings and set us on an unchangeable path in which all of our daily actions and consequences are predetermined. God invites us to choose good rather than evil. I believe that God rejoices when we choose to live with good intent and that God grieves our poor choices. No matter the reaction of God, we remain free to choose. God does not program us to act or to react or to respond in ways decided long before the present moment. In every situation, we freely choose our course of action. Some choices are straightforward while other choices need consideration of multiple factors. Sometimes we choose well and other times unwisely. Sometimes our choice becomes a reaction because of our emotional state. (I think of the frazzled and fatigued parent who reacts angrily to the exuberance and enthusiasm of a preschool child.) Sometimes we choose to stop and to look more rationally at the choices before us. No matter how we decide to act, the choice remains ours. Think about this freedom to choose as a gift. I believe that this gift of freedom also involves love and trust on God's part. The love comes out of that longed-for relationship that God wants with all people. God's trust grows from the hope that we will choose wisely. For this gift of free choice I am thankful.

Think about Hammarskjold's prayer for all that has been and all that will be. What events do you identify as high points? How did you think about God's presence in those moments? Thanking God for those high points is a wonderful exercise in remembrance. We remember a variety of moments that range from a special evening to a particular celebration. These celebrations may have religious connections or they may relate to a school event or a friendship. Enjoy a time of remembering these high moments in life.

One ordinary day in the month of June when I lived in Nashville, I planned to go to the office and there prepare for a convention of booksellers. After a time of devotional reading and prayer, I went for my morning walk-run. I always began my morning run by walking. I'm not much of a runner. I don't simply jump up and run. I usually walk five or six blocks before I feel ready to run. Even after warming up, I grunt and groan and stumble through each run and my body never stops protesting. I left the house that morning, walked up and over and down a railroad overpass, and then started a long walk on a straight and level street in a residential area. A few birds whistled. A fence (thankfully) contained a large mixed-breed dog that always showed lots of interest as I went by. A cat balanced on a fence in search of prey. The wind rustled shrubs and trees. As I breathed, I expressed gratitude for this beautiful morning of ordinary awe. I felt gratitude for the morning beauty, the relatively cool temperature, and the sense of normalcy in the neighborhood. Gratitude grew from being able to walk and then to run.

Then I noticed four young men walking in the middle of the street toward me. They seemed to spread farther apart as they approached me and covered the width of the roadway. I thought that I would walk past them. I still was not ready to run. (A little background: During years of living and walking in one of the urban centers of Nashville, I encountered a number of street people and dealt kindly with them. Once a man asked for money for food. "I don't have any money, but I'll be glad to take you to my church—it's a block away—where I can get you some food." "No, but I thank you. You've treated me like a human being. You didn't ignore me.")

We continued to move closer to one another. They seemed young. I began to feel odd intuitive warnings. I wondered if I should reverse course and go the other way. *No, I'll just go through them.* The four teens blocked my way. I did not know them. I would not recognize or know them today.

"Hey, do you have a cigarette?" These four appeared to be fourteen to sixteen years old.

"No, I'm going on a run. Why would I have a cigarette?"

I only began that second sentence. One member of the group hit me hard in the nose and then another punch followed and I was on the ground while one or more of the group kicked me. I felt only kicks and a spreading numbness. I heard no sounds. Perhaps dogs barked and birds whistled and cats still stalked and the wind rustled the vegetation, but I did not experience any of nature's beauty that I had admired moments before. I began to hear my own voice, "Why? Why?" I realized that I had curled into a fetal position with arms protecting my head.

Then I heard a loud male voice. "Hey! Leave that guy alone! I'm getting my phone and calling the cops."

The four ran away. The man helped me to the curb and sat with me until police and emergency personnel arrived. The police took a report and the emergency personnel checked vital signs and loaded me into an ambulance. At the hospital doctors did an MRI, sewed eight stitches in my eyelid, took care of my broken nose, and discovered some damage to my right arm from the kicks.

After telephone calls to find a ride home from the hospital and to inform my team at work, I noticed the sky remained blue. I'd like to tell you that I offered a prayer of gratitude then for the rescue, but I did not. *Why?* I prayed. *Why did this happen? What did I do to cause this to happen?* How quickly blame comes from within! I began to address these questions with a mental health counselor. If I were to meet those four assailants today, I would still ask the same question: *Why? What was the purpose of the attack? What did you expect to gain?* My tone of voice now is different than it was then. I do not sense the anguish of that time. My questions now grow from a sense of curiosity.

Some moments seem never to generate gratitude. Some portions of life seem devoid of thanksgiving, and yet we may discover the gift of gratitude when we look back on these harsh times. I cannot thank God for an assault on the street, but I cannot hold God responsible for that action. Human beings remain free to choose. I remain grateful for the unknown stranger who intervened during that attack. The one who intervened when I was attacked made a decision, though he had several choices. He could have remained silent and let the attack persist. He could have returned violence with violence. He could have called the police from inside his home and hidden there. He chose to call the police and to confront the attackers and then to sit with me and to keep me relatively calm and alert until the police and medical personnel arrived. After I had healed enough to go back to the block where I was attacked, I knocked at the doors of the houses to find and thank this man who called the police and sat with me. No one claimed to have called the police. No one knew the person I described. This mysterious intervention still puzzles me, and I continue to express gratitude for the stranger. Here I have more questions than answers: Was this person someone passing by? Was this interventionist a messenger of God? Whoever or whatever he was, I am glad that he made the choice to intervene.

What do you identify as bleak and low points in the fabric of life? Whether those moments were death or divorce or some other disruption, how do you think about God in those moments? Is it possible for you to look back at the ups and downs of your life and gratefully say the first line of Hammarskjold's prayer? Before you offer that too-quick affirmation, consider the less than grand experiences of your life. Remember the hard and difficult and boring times, and remember the celebrations. Each choice leads to another choice, and so our lives grow through the variety of moments and experiences. As we pray Hammarskjold's prayer, we begin to see the fullness of our lives and how each friendship and event and conversation interweaves with another and still another. We begin better to understand the connectivity of our days, and for the ups and downs and the times when we sit sideways, we continue to live with gratitude.

The Uncertain Future

"To all that shall be—Yes!"

We embark on an expedition in life, and the adventure takes us into places of wonder and enchantment. We go into places or situations in which we serve the needs of others. We may become agents of healing—like the one who intervened on the street for me—and we may become people, like Dag Hammarskjold, who work for reconciliation.

We make plans for life. Consider that ordinary June day on which I was attacked. My calendar showed several meetings and planned telephone calls. None happened, and the organization survived. Our calendars contain notes about this or that activity and course of action. Some of us schedule meetings a year in advance. Some of us plan an approach to life in which we attempt to amass tremendous wealth. Others plan to live in simple ways. Woody Allen famously said, "If you want to make God laugh, tell him your plans."

Daily life unfolds before us as a series of questions for the future: What will I experience? Who will I meet? What will surprise me today? What will challenge me? How will I make decisions and choices?

Gregory of Nyssa, fourth-century Greek theologian, wrote, "Concepts create idols; only wonder grasps anything" (*The Life of Moses*). If we strive and struggle only to fulfill our own plans, we will not notice God's invitation to wonder and delight in the creation and in the love of God.

These questions lead us to the large questions: What is God's will? Does God have a plan for me? As I write this section, I am aware of one company that currently uses a variation of these two questions to promote a religious dating service. Their service will help the user find "the one God intends." When I think of the will of God, I do not understand it to apply to each moment and each decision of each day. (I write more about this will of God in **Chapter 3, The Rabbi's Prayer**.) God does not predetermine each action of our lives. God does not turn us into androids like Data of *Star Trek: The Next Generation* and we thus act only as God determines. We make choices each day, and our choices are made freely. Our friends and families influence our choices. What we read or see or hear will influence our choices. Yesterday's decisions influence today's choices and decisions. In the midst of our need to make decisions among these many choices, we seek guidance from God.

I think that the will of God begins with God's longing for relationship with each of us. Beyond that, the will of God means God's dream for us. I believe that a part of God's dream is that we will develop and use our gifts and abilities to serve the greater needs of the world: to serve justice, to do what is right, to care for orphans and widows, to feed the hungry, to clothe the naked, to heal the sick, to visit those in prison, and to love what God loves. I believe that God loves the world and wants the world to thrive in a way similar to the way that we may want our friends and families to thrive and blossom. Growing in love with God and with God's creation is the will of God as I understand it.

Wendy Wright, Roman Catholic theologian and spiritual director, described a retreat in which one of the participants spoke to her about understanding the will of God. The participant said, "For years I've been asking people wherever I go, how do I know God's will for my life? No one ever gave me a good answer until recently, and I want to share that answer with you. . . . If you think you can see God's will laid out neatly before you for the next five, ten, or twenty years as a clearly defined path, this is emphatically not the will of God. But if you sense that the next hesitant step you are about to make into an uncertain future is somehow directed by God, that is most probably God's will for you" (Wright in *Companions in Christ Participant's Book*, pp. 235–236).

How does this connect with Hammarskjold's prayer? Every step into the uncertainty of the future is an affirmation, a Yes! to God. I do not know from moment to moment what will happen in my life, and even less do I know what will happen in your life, but

I do trust that God loves us even as we go somewhat hesitantly into the uncertain future.

Star Trek VI: The Undiscovered Country, which shows up on cable television nearly every other weekend, made much of the soliloquy from Hamlet. Despite the humor of Chancellor Gorkon's statement, "You haven't heard Shakespeare until you've heard it in the original Klingon," I think the English language serves us well:

> But that the dread of something after death,
> The undiscovered country, from whose
>   bourn
> No traveller returns, puzzles the will . . . .
>   (*Hamlet*, Act III, Scene 1)

Hamlet struggles with the meaning of life and the suffering that happens to all people. The character decides that death is preferable to the long-suffering toil and frustration of life, and yet he does not commit suicide, though it seems to him a logical way beyond the suffering. He chooses not to take such action because that act would take him to the undiscovered country. You and I may not think of our journeys into the undiscovered country in the way that Hamlet did. Our undiscovered country may simply be the next chapter of work or relationship or connection with others. We do stumble our way through life. Even the most well-planned lives are filled with unplanned moments and interruptions. Uncertainty happens all the time, and our best course of action becomes one of trust in the constancy of God's love.

I want to return to the mystery of those falls I experienced. I explained to the doctor that, after a number of falls, I experienced something like convulsions and wondered if I experienced epileptic seizures. The doctor eliminated epilepsy, but felt the convulsions were significant. He began to suspect a heart problem, and I went through many heart tests. The stress tests, echocardiography, EKG, Tilt Table Testing, and Holter Monitor showed no problems. An electrophysiologist inserted an internal heart monitor. After three months with that bionic device, the medical team learned that my heart was stopping for eight to ten seconds and then self-starting. The after-fall convulsions came when my heart started itself anew. The heart stoppage did not happen often nor did it happen when I was driving nor did it happen during those medical tests, but the internal monitor showed that my heart stopped and the falls were one consequence. I now have another bionic device connected to three of my four heart chambers. I return to the electrophysiologist regularly for his team to check the battery life of my device. He then tells me that all is well and that I should grow much older.

Maybe that will be true. I know that when I convulsed back to life after those heart stoppages, I felt a difference in perspective. I did not see flashing lights or the brilliant white light described by those who have near-death experiences or life after death experiences. I simply experienced a different sensation. During the year of testing and surgeries, the certainty of death became more clear to me. The uncertain gift of time continues to become a wonder.

To say yes to all that shall be requires courage. We do not know how life will unfold. Will we experience disease? Possibly. Will we experience disappointments because of work? Probably. Will we experience the death of a relationship? Very likely. Will we face obstacles and challenges and moments of extraordinary strain in the future? Absolutely.

Sometimes people voice a large question that travels with the question concerning the will of God. This question comes from our experience of tragedy. Whether we witness the destruction of tornado or tsunami or the violence of acts of terrorism or a school shooting or the genocidal efforts to eliminate a people and a culture, questions surface: Where was God and how could God let this happen? First, separate natural disasters from the violence unleashed by human beings. While we grow in our understanding of weather patterns and climate change or the impact of a tectonic plate shift beneath the Pacific Ocean, we continue to ask the question of relationship and the connection between our scientific understanding and our theological perspective. Knowledge of the cause of natural disaster does not remove from us the mysterious and mystical questions concerning life on earth.

Our prayers do not manipulate God. I do not believe that God suspends the laws of physics or geography. We offer prayers concerning these disasters in the time before and in the time after the events. We may pray that God will spare our lives and our loved ones. Often that happens; we live through the natural disaster and our lives return to normal. We also pray after the event for survivors and rescue workers, and we mourn the loss of life.

In April 1998 a tornado damaged my eastside neighborhood in Nashville. One person died and only that one person, a gifted college student, but the tornado impacted many lives. That tornado brought the gift of clarity to people who struggled with problems that had seemed insoluble prior to the tornado. Change happened as a consequence of that tornado. Did God allow that storm to happen so that people could face their issues? Certainly not! Or, as some publicity seekers claim whenever a natural disaster occurs, did that tornado become punishment for the neighborhood? Absolutely not! A God who loves the created world and all who live on earth would not select a random neighborhood or town for punishment. That simply does not fit my understanding of God's generous mercy. We live in a created order, and my understanding of order is that of a system that grows from actions and reactions and consequences that lead to other actions and reactions. Did God help people discover clarity after the fact? The crisis experience gave people a different sense of time and need, helping people to sort out their priorities and goals. We pray in the storms of life—environmental or emotional—and our prayers seek connection with God for support, hope, and love.

How do we deal with the calamities or catastrophes caused by other human beings? Individuals go on violent rampages, killing those whom the perpetrators did not know. We struggle to make sense of the random and senseless violence, ending with an answer that does not satisfy the question. We have witnessed too many photos of hunger, photos of genocide and other crimes against humanity. Parts of my family survived the genocide of Armenians in the Ottoman Empire. Parts of my family died in the forced desert march around Deir es-Zor during that effort to remove all traces of the Armenian people from modern Turkey. My father's two older brothers, both under the age of ten, died during that genocide. My father's family could not speak about the pain of the dead boys nor could my mother's family speak of the deaths of their relatives during the genocide.

Raphael Lemkin defined genocide in his 1944 publication *Axis Rule in Occupied Europe*, concerning crimes against international law. It was in this work that Lemkin coined the word *genocide* to describe what happened to the Armenian people; the United Nations adopted Lemkin's definition in 1948 as part of its Convention on the Prevention and Punishment of the Crime of Genocide. Genocide is a systematic effort to destroy all signs of an ethnic people or culture. We witnessed such crimes against humanity in places as diverse as Tibet, Iraq, Bosnia, Rwanda, and Cambodia.

The perpetrators of these heinous crimes offer highly implausible arguments to justify their actions. Adolph Hitler repeated the Ottoman accusations concerning the Armenians when he began the Jewish Holocaust. Evil always seeks to rationalize and justify itself.

I cannot explain the madness that underlies genocidal efforts. I can only turn to a most basic answer about the human condition. We have choice, and we are free to choose between doing good or doing evil. Just as you and I can choose directions for our lives, all other human beings are free to make their own choices. Some people choose to contribute positively to life. Others choose actions that devolve and destroy; however, the answer is not as simple as individual choice. While I know that individuals may choose to act in moral ways, I recognize that groups of individuals or societies may choose to act in ways that differ from the individual path. In 1932 the ethicist Reinhold Niebuhr introduced his study of politics and ethics entitled *Moral Man and Immoral Society* with these words:

> [A] sharp distinction must be drawn between the moral and social behavior of individuals and of social groups, national, racial, and economic; and that this distinction justifies and necessitates political policies which a purely individualistic ethic must always find embarrassing. (Niebuhr, xi)

His understanding, which may at first seem quaint in the twenty-first century, remains sharply perceptive. Niebuhr focused on the evil of social systems, a formidable task that we need to recall as we deal with the problems of nationhood and the issues that go beyond national sovereignty, such as multinational corporations and multinational lobbying entities. While Niebuhr focused on the political realm, his work continues to inform my ethical understanding of individuals and groups. Niebuhr's perspective on individuals and the collective body grew from his understanding of human nature and sin. He accepted the idea that individuals could go beyond self-interest in their daily relationships and transactions, but nations or classes of people could not transcend self-interest. Because of this inability of the state or corporate entity, Niebuhr observed that nations often do not understand the harm or injustice that they create through their actions. He grounds his hope in Christian love (agape), but his analysis remains somewhat cynical; Niebuhr's political analysis remains a helpful perspective for us as we deal with political violence. His answers do not solve the problem of our inhumanity toward one another, but they offer a basis to begin our own spiritual wrangling with the question.

While I hope that all my actions are moral and for the good, I do not have vision to foresee the consequences of my actions. I make a decision. I act in good faith—not in a legal sense, but in a hope that my actions are right for the circumstances. I make each choice in the knowledge that I am stepping gingerly in faith. In a way, I join with John Climacus who, around the year 600, wrote a treatise concerning religious virtues and used the metaphor of an ascending ladder to describe the journey. Each step leads to the next. Each decision leads to the next. Each choice leads to the next choice, and no matter what we know about the decision or choice, we still move into unknown territory.

To say yes, as Hammarskjold invites us, to all that shall be calls us to set aside fear of the unknown, particularly the future. When I read the Bible, many passages surprise me still because their message includes the words, "Do not fear" or "Be not afraid." In many of these passages, the one addressed is in a position of weakness, either as the recipient of an angelic visitor (see Genesis 15:1–6 when old Abram is told "Do not be afraid" and is promised offspring; Genesis 26:23–25, when Isaac receives the message of blessing; Genesis 46:1–4 in which Jacob is told to not fear; Exodus 20:20 when Moses delivers the Ten Commandments; Matthew 1:18–25 or Luke 1:26–38) or more simply as someone oppressed by religious persecution (see the New Testament epistles). Jesus offered these words to his followers in his farewell discourse: "Do not let your hearts be troubled, and do not let them be afraid" (John 14:27), a verse that easily becomes a breath prayer. In these situations, the salutation reminds the listener to not fear and to know that God offers love and liberation. No matter whether the greeting addresses Abram or Moses or Peter or Mary and other women at the tomb, an assurance of peace and encouragement to step into the unknown happens. These biblical moments speak to our everyday experiences. I think that we receive encouragement to step into the unknown of each day and each future. We hear that encouragement through our communities of friends and communities of believers, and we hear that encouragement through reading the Bible, and we hear encouragement during the times in which we pray and listen silently for God's direction.

The other side of the Yes to the future is that God says Yes to us. God affirms and loves each of us as we are. God does not condemn us, but God loves us. I do not know of a larger or greater Yes than that.

As we move into the future, we remember all that has been part of our lives and we offer gratitude; and with each new day we affirm its creative possibility and our relationship with God.

For all that has been—Thanks!

To all that shall be—Yes!

Prayer

2

Ensemble: The Theologian's Prayer

As an eight-year-old I noticed a small wooden plaque on my mother's desk next to her even-then old Underwood manual typewriter (with black and red cloth ribbon). The plaque contained a short form of the Serenity Prayer: "God, grant me Serenity to accept what I cannot change, Courage to change what I can, and Wisdom to know the difference."

"What's serenity?" I asked.

"It means an inner calm."

"You're always calm."

"Ah, you're a wonderful boy, but you don't know what it takes to be calm. When you grow up, you'll understand these words better."

Her prediction certainly proved correct, and I also understood far better what she meant when she indicated that internal struggle. My parents' marriage did not demonstrate any attributes of a good or happy marriage. My father extended tremendous generosity to friends and customers in his business, but with the family he embodied the truth of an old Armenian proverb: "He's so cheap he takes seven bites from a raisin." Passive-aggressive behavior and more active domestic violence ruled family life. My mother also faced breast cancer. She was released from the hospital after a radical mastectomy two days before the assassination of President John Kennedy and so those two events are inextricably linked in my memory.

That plaque remained next to that Underwood typewriter on my mother's desk until her death in 1984, and I imagine that she read and prayed those words often.

I later began to experience the depth of the Serenity Prayer in small-group settings. The experience of praying these words with others in a supportive group setting began to confirm my mother's wisdom and to reanimate that prayer tradition in my life.

The Pastor-Theologian

Few people today know the name of Reinhold Niebuhr. Many more people know and use his words on a daily basis. I find much in the life of Reinhold

Niebuhr with which to identify. Niebuhr's parents immigrated to the United States from Germany. His father was a German-speaking pastor in Missouri and Illinois. The family spoke German inside their home in the same way that my family spoke Armenian within the home.

After his ordination in 1915, Reinhold began pastoral ministry in the city of Detroit. Detroit then was a much different city from the bankrupt city of the early twenty-first century. Henry Ford, Walter Chrysler, Horace and John Dodge, James Packard, and others had turned the city into the prosperous headquarters of the American automobile industry. People migrated from across the United States to Detroit to find jobs. Detroit became the fourth largest city in the United States with large Roman Catholic and Jewish populations in addition to African-Americans and Caucasians from the South. One reaction to this mix of industry, population growth, and cultural change was the growth of the Ku Klux Klan in Detroit.

Niebuhr first ministered at a church that numbered about 65 people in 1915. When he left in 1928 to teach at New York's Union Theological Seminary, the church had approximately 700 members. During his Detroit years, Niebuhr addressed social concerns and the needs of workers in the factories. After leaving the church, Niebuhr put together a small book titled *Leaves from the Notebook of a Tamed Cynic* in which he pulled together entries from his journals during the Detroit years. The title alone reveals the essence of Reinhold Niebuhr. While his cynical side may have been tamed, he remained a Christian skeptic and astute observer of culture and Christianity.

In the preface to *Leaves*, Niebuhr wrote:

> The modern ministry is in no easy position; for it is committed to the espousal of ideals (professionally, at that) which are in direct conflict with the dominant interests and prejudices of contemporary civilization. This conflict is nowhere more apparent than in America, where neither ancient sanctities nor new social insights tend to qualify, as they do in Europe, the heedless economic forces of an industrial era. Inevitably a compromise must be made, or is made, between the rigor of the ideal and the necessities of the day. (vii)

His comments do not seem especially radical now, but in 1929 Niebuhr's words threatened many people as the work of a militant.

During the Detroit years and throughout his years teaching in seminary, Niebuhr addressed a number of social concerns from a theological perspective. In the 1930s, he spoke and wrote about how *hubris*— the sin of pride—was the basic evil in the world. In the depth of the Great Depression then occurring, such an explanation resonated with many. Later still in his lectures and speeches and books, Niebuhr argued with both liberals and conservatives, calling religious liberals naïve because they did not take seriously the pervasive nature of sin and evil and fighting religious conservatives because he felt their perspectives on the Bible were dim-witted and their understanding of "true religion" demonstrated a lack of understanding of God's compassion and grace. Because Niebuhr wrote much and spoke more often, addressing a variety of ills and evils, both liberals and conservatives claim him, which is proof to me that Reinhold Niebuhr cannot be neatly pigeonholed or placed in a box. Categorize Niebuhr if you must as a progressive, but recognize that Niebuhr's progressive understanding differs from contemporary understandings of progressive theology or politics. Throughout his lifetime, Niebuhr offered theological and ethical commentary on political policy in the public forum. That willingness to comment and to challenge conventional wisdom is part of my own affinity with Reinhold Niebuhr.

Setting the Prayer in Time and Circumstance

Many of us have read the Serenity Prayer on a wall plaque or a poster, and we may have prayed these words with others in a group. Here is the brief form of Reinhold Niebuhr's prayer:

> God, grant me the serenity to accept the
>   things I cannot change,
> Courage to change the things I can change,
> And wisdom to know the difference.
> Amen.

The short version is easy to remember and is meaningful to the many who have joined in praying it in support and twelve-step groups. People assume that the Serenity Prayer is old—I suspect because it offers a perspective that seems rare today. I continue to see people react in surprise when they learn that the prayer originated in the twentieth century.

Context provides a key to understanding a prayer, an essay, or an action. In her memoir *The Serenity Prayer: Faith and Politics in Times of Peace and War*, Elisabeth Sifton, daughter of Reinhold and Ursula Niebuhr, describes the circumstances during which the prayer was written. Sifton introduces the prayer by first telling us what it is not:

> People usually presume that it's very old,
> for its stringency and spiritual clarity seem
> unusual for our soupy, compromised times.
> It's surely rabbinical in origin, or Stoic,
> derived or translated from Latin or Hebrew,
> maybe Scottish. . . . How dramatic the irony,

then, that the actual author was an American
of German descent who wrote the prayer in
the United States in 1943, at the height of
the war against Germany . . . . (*The Serenity
Prayer*, pp. 9–10)

Because context provides a key to understanding,
I want to look at the context in which Niebuhr wrote
the prayer and to draw some parallels between that
time and our own. Niebuhr wrote the prayer in the
midst of a world war. In 1939, Adolf Hitler began his
effort to conquer the world and to usher in the thou-
sand-year reign of National Socialism. World War II
brought together the Axis Powers of Germany, Italy,
and Japan, plus some nations conquered by these
three. Opposed to the Axis powers were the Allied
Forces of the United Kingdom, France, Poland,
Belgium, Brazil, China, Czechoslovakia, Ethiopia,
Greece, India, Mexico, the Netherlands, Norway,
Yugoslavia, the Soviet Union, and the United States.
Allied leaders, including democratic republics and
communist nations, understood the harsh threat of
Adolf Hitler's fascist and evil effort to dominate and
control the world. The warfare was brutal throughout
many areas of the world. Scholars disagree on the
number of deaths that resulted from this war. Military
deaths range from 22 to 25 million, including deaths
of about 5 million prisoners of war. Civilian death
estimates range from 38 to 55 million, including 13
to 20 million from war-related disease and famine.

In the United States preparation for the war included the groundbreaking for The Pentagon on September 11, 1941. (Was this September 11 date also a part of the rationale in setting the date of the 2001 terrorist attacks?) Officials dedicated the Pentagon on January 15, 1943.

Reinhold Niebuhr struggled in the lead-up to U.S. involvement in the war. He had long opposed the rise of National Socialism in Germany. He had spoken out against Hitler. Other American pastors felt secure in thinking that the relative isolation of the United States would keep the nation safe from Hitler. Niebuhr instead called for American intervention in the coming war and argued against all forms of totalitarianism; yet, Niebuhr the pastor understood the destruction of war and that families would lose loved ones to the fighting. While Niebuhr saw clearly the evil of Hitler, he also understood the costs of war. I look across the United States today and see how terrible a price our nation is paying because of our involvement in two somewhat localized wars; these two military actions are leading the nation, I fear, to a national state of permanent war. Indeed, some legislators with whom I disagree think that that United States withdrew too soon from Iraq and Afghanistan.

During the second world war, President Franklin Roosevelt enacted wage and price freezes to prevent inflation. In the United States, civilians needed ration coupons to buy gasoline, tires, and certain

foods such as meat, sugar, butter, milk, and pro-
cessed foods. Civilians also needed ration coupons to
buy typewriters, bicycles, and silk when or if these
durable goods were available. In October 1942 the
U.S. government established a national speed limit of
35 miles per hour to save gasoline and tires. Because
of the scarcity of rubber and the need to have ration
coupons and money, people drove on tires that were
patched many times over. Those who lived through
this war felt that it lasted an eternity.

One of Roosevelt's domestic policies created a
rift in this nation. Because of the fear that swept the
nation, the President issued an executive order to
establish internment camps for Japanese-Americans
on the West Coast. The government put over 110,000
Japanese-Americans into these guarded living centers. In 1988 President Reagan issued a statement of
apology to Japanese-Americans for the internment
camps, blaming prejudice, war hysteria, and a failure
of political leadership for the camps. The government
also interned about 11,000 Americans of German
ancestry. Fear won that battle, and we continue to
deal with similar fears.

Even before World War II began, theologies
and social philosophies clashed in very public ways.
The 1930s began with the Great Depression (while
it officially started in 1929, analysts see the roots of
that economic calamity beginning much earlier in
the 1920s). President Calvin Coolidge (1923–1929)
practiced a very passive style of leadership because of

his belief in small government. He, along with his Treasury Secretary Andrew Mellon, believed in the form of economics known as "trickle-down." Herbert Hoover, a Republican like Coolidge, became President after Coolidge and continued similar policies. His campaign rejected subsidies for farms, supported prohibition, and pledged lower taxes. Hoover's policies could not deal effectively with the impact of the economic crisis that became the Great Depression. Prior to the stock market crash in October 1929, the federal government raised interest rates to restrict credit buying. U.S. industrial production began falling in 1929. As the depression continued throughout the world, people's expectations began to change, and by 1931 many people felt that their lives would only grow worse and whatever money or wealth they had would soon become worthless. In 1932 the country felt that the change promised by Franklin Delano Roosevelt would bring national recovery. Despite the hope proclaimed by Roosevelt's theme song "Happy Day Are Here Again," only the 1941 intervention in World War II began to lift the United States from the economic disaster known as the Great Depression.

In the 1930s biblical literalists attacked those they deemed as liberal, including Niebuhr and other progressive pastor-theologians, such as the American Baptist preacher Harry Emerson Fosdick and Bishop Francis J. McConnell of the Methodist Episcopal

Church. Emboldened by the efforts of William Jennings Bryan in the 1925 Scopes Trial in Tennessee, these biblical literalists continued their attacks on those persons they described as "unbiblical" because they did not hold to a list of proscribed beliefs that included the inspiration of the Bible and the inerrancy of scripture as a result of this understanding.

I see many parallels between that era and our own time. Among those parallels, the most debilitating factor is fear itself, which had a strong rebirth after the terrorist attacks of September 11. Instead of interning Japanese-Americans, some voices began to call for the internment or imprisonment of anyone of Middle Eastern background or any speaker of Arabic. Strangers and co-workers labeled my Armenian Christian friends as Islamic terrorists—despite the reality that my friends came as refugees from genocidal efforts in Azerbaijan ten years earlier. Fear unleashed hatred, and hatred is always irrational.

Because of the union of wealth with conservative political and theological thought, we are engaged in a strange and somewhat nonsensical debate concerning science and pseudo-science, which mirrors the Scopes Trial. Our nation moved within fifteen years from a period of relative prosperity, similar to the 1920s with surplus funds in the federal budget, to a recession and a grave federal financial deficit. We learned that our financial institutions were "too big to fail" while individuals were failing all over the land.

Today in the United States, a variety of voices engage in very public debates on how best to achieve the common good of individuals, the nation, and the world. Conflicting views on social philosophy, the role of the state, the relationship between church and state, and other concerns remain a part of our national debate. Some voices base their arguments on the interests of business; what is good and most profitable for business becomes their only concern. Other voices speak of concerns for the rights of individuals as superior to that of corporate entities. Still other voices argue that the nation needs a better sense of purpose and the common good. We debate the purpose of public education, the place of science, and what or how to teach science. We try to legislate decisions, behavior, conduct, and choices made by people. I hear a cacophony of voices blaring against one another with very little clarity in conversations critical for our present and future. In the midst of such dissonance, serenity calls us to use language to heal wounds rather than inflict new ones.

In 1991 I worked with an editorial team member who came to the United States from China in the months after the 1989 Tiananmen Square demonstrations. Mr. Zhuang left because he was known to have translated speeches of Vaclav Havel concerning freedom and individual rights into Mandarin Chinese. One day we talked about the student demonstrations at Tiananmen Square. He said, "You cannot understand China until you understand

how much we are indoctrinated by Mao's Little
Red Book. Everyone in China knows it. We must
memorize it from childhood." He told me that one
form of protest at Tiananmen Square was to wear a
t-shirt imprinted with the number that referred to
Chairman Mao's statement about the importance of
education. No other words appeared on the shirt,
and Chinese people knew that the number referred
to education. The United States does not have such
a glossary of common experience for our political-
ethical conversation. Engaging in our national polit-
ical-ethical conversation calls for careful statements
and careful listening and careful questions. I hope
that we will embrace genuine conversational dialogue around the questions of national purpose, the
common good, the intersection of our various free-
doms with national security interests, and individual
rights and the larger public interest. These conversations need to happen in every generation in the midst
of changing technologies and other frontiers in our
common life.

The alliance of fear and uncertainty offers the
greatest affinity between Niebuhr's era and our own
time. Given the daily reports of "threat levels" and
the constant reports of terrorism and violence, we
risk falling prey to a permanent state of fear and anxiety. When we are tempted to give up in the face
this unhappy alliance, we waken our non-anxious
presence and strength through meditation upon the
Serenity Prayer.

Unfolding the Serenity Prayer

While a tremendous gift, the short version of the Serenity Prayer does not give us the depth of Niebuhr's prayer. Against the background in which Niebuhr wrote the Serenity Prayer and the noise of our own time, read now the full version of the prayer:

> God, give me grace to accept with serenity
> the things that cannot be changed,
> Courage to change the things
> which should be changed,
> and the Wisdom to distinguish
> the one from the other.
> Living one day at a time,
> Enjoying one moment at a time,
> Accepting hardship as a pathway to peace,
> Taking, as Jesus did,
> This sinful world as it is,
> Not as I would have it,
> Trusting that You will make all things right,
> If I surrender to Your will,
> So that I may be reasonably happy in this life,
> And supremely happy with You forever in
>   the next.
> Amen.

I invite you to read again the full version of the prayer. Read it slowly or meditatively and give the words time to soak into your head and your heart.

The first two lines may be the most familiar, but Reinhold Niebuhr uses words that may not be part of our common understanding. The first word is grace. You may know an adult who asks a child to "say grace." Grace may refer to a short prayer before a meal, and even that usage points to a deeper meaning of the word. Think of grace as holy, undeserved mercy. Think of grace as a gift that we do nothing to earn. Theologians refer to grace as the unmerited love of God given to humanity for their regeneration or sanctification. For Niebuhr, grace remains at the heart of all life. I first came to Niebuhr, as did many, by reading his dark understanding of sin. Niebuhr gave a series of lectures at the University of Edinburgh in 1939, and these lectures became the basis of his two-volume publication titled *The Nature and Destiny of Man*. Niebuhr's cynicism still comes through as he describes sin and evil, and many people seemed to understand that Niebuhr felt pessimistic at best about humanity. The more we read Niebuhr, the more we realize that he understood grace as the divine power in humanity, and this divine power extended love and mercy and healing. Niebuhr believed that this mercy of God was far more powerful than any sinfulness of humanity. Understanding grace in this way meant, for Niebuhr, that grace embraced truth and justice and love. This love, for Niebuhr, means the Christian understanding of *agape* or sacrificial love and not a romantic understanding. This understanding of grace in its multidimensionality provides the possibility of living within a civil society: truth, sacrificial love, and justice become portions of grace, the gift of God's presence in our lives.

I hope that paragraph on grace does not seem too heavy. I think that we need to understand the basis for the prayer. In many ways Niebuhr reminds us that God is affirming and redeeming humanity despite the mistakes we humans make in our deeds and in our thinking.

When we pray, "God, give me grace," we invite the Holy One to open us to the mystery of life in the fullness of truth, love, and justice. We also invite the divine power of God within us to guide our actions in truth, love, and justice.

God, give me grace to accept with serenity the things that cannot be changed. I do not think that Niebuhr invites passivity; however, I think it helpful to consider what we cannot change in our lives. I think back to my mother in that marriage. She tried a number of ways to change the marriage relationship. She went to secular and pastoral counselors. At least one counselor visited with my father in his business in an attempt to intervene. My mother considered divorce in a time when divorce was not accepted, and she gave in to the conventional wisdom to stay married because of the family. She did not endure the marriage in passive resignation. She found ways to express herself through art and music, through gardening. She also sought the power of meditation and prayer to deal with the situation. She learned to speak lovingly in her own voice to find ways to help others deal with relational issues.

I invite you to make a list of the things you cannot change as you say the first words of the Serenity Prayer. I offer these general examples to start the process: I cannot change the weather, though I certainly pray about it. I cannot change or fix other people, though I pray always for them. I cannot directly change national social policies, though I pray and act for certain issues—but I'm beginning to veer from this portion of the prayer.

> God, the gift of peacefulness,
> of inner calm, of feeling untroubled
> as I recognize those matters in the midst
>   of life
> that I cannot refashion in my own vision
>   or image.

The first sentence of this prayer can become a confession as we name those things that we would like to change and yet recognize that we are powerless to change. The gift of this sentence is the recognition that we need not shoulder responsibility for everything happening in the world.

Courage to change the things which should be changed. Niebuhr understood grace as embracing truth, justice, and love. When we pray these words, we also begin to see the brokenness in our lives and invite God's power to help us bring that change within our lives. We cannot change other people, but we can grow and change ourselves, our responses and circumstances. This phrase invites us to recognize that the divine power invites us to wholeness and to health. Such wholeness may mean changes to bring emotional or physical or spiritual or relational health. As we pray the Serenity Prayer, truth, justice, and love become the lens through which we see the world. While we cannot fix others, we need not accept the conditions that generate brokenness. We strive to change social conditions or policies or cultural understandings for the sake of justice and love. We pray for courage to act, and we continue to invite God to give us this courage to change because courage is as much a gift as the serenity for which we ask.

. . . *and the Wisdom to distinguish the one from the other.* We invoke the divine grace to know the difference between what to accept and what to change. How do you understand wisdom? Sometimes people use words interchangeably even though the words have different meanings. I think many people confuse knowledge and wisdom. Think of knowledge as the collection of facts or skills or information about a given area. We may know a lot about one or more subjects. Think of wisdom as a merging of knowledge, action, and principle. Wisdom gathers our knowledge of a subject and adds a depth perception of people, things, and/or situations. Wisdom then connects these varied points of information, including perception, with our knowledge of an area. Some writers believe that true wisdom comes from setting aside one's emotions in order to analyze more fully the possibility. The Vulcans of the Star Trek universe exhibit this non-emotional category of wisdom, but humans are less able to separate our emotions from other processes of understanding. No matter where we stand in emotional or other intelligence (and here I applaud Howard Gardner in defining nine types of intelligence[1]), this phrase continues to emphasize the divine gift of grace to discern: the gift to put together deep understanding, possibility, potential, and discretion. We pray for wisdom to understand the difference between those people and situations that we cannot change and those situations that we can, but our emphasis in this prayer still brings us

---

1 Howard Gardner included these types of intelligence: naturalist (the ability to discriminate among living things), musical (the ability to discern pitch, rhythm, tone), logical-mathematical (the ability to calculate, consider propositions, analyze, and use abstract and symbolic thought), existential (the ability to tackle deep questions about human existence), interpersonal (the ability to understand and interact well or effectively with others), bodily-kinesthetic (the ability to use physical skills), linguistic (the ability to think in words and to use language), intra-personal (the ability to understand oneself and one's feelings and thoughts), spatial (the ability to think in three dimensions). For more information, see Howard E. Gardner, *Frames of Mind: The Theory of Multiple Intelligences* (New York: Basic Books, 1983) and also Gardner's additional development of the theory in *Intelligence Reframed: Multiple Intelligence For The 21st Century* (New York: Basic Books, 1999).

back to gift. We are praying for the grace or gift to understand this difference.

Still we pray for a sense of discernment to understand this difference. Discernment is also a peculiar aspect of wisdom and serenity. While discernment is usually defined as an ability to perceive or to judge well, I use discernment here as a larger process of understanding. How is it that we begin to discern the distinctions noted by this prayer between the things we can change and the things we cannot? We call upon the divine power of God at work within us. To discern is to listen, and I invite you to take time now to stop reading and to invite God's presence by praying as a breath prayer this phrase from the Serenity Prayer: "the wisdom to distinguish the one from the other." Your breathing rhythm will determine the musical flow of the prayer. One natural way is to inhale and to pray "the wisdom to distinguish" and to exhale and pray "the one from the other." Take your time and let the breath prayer flow. This book should still be here when you return.

If you stopped reading for prayer, what mental images came to you? Do any of these images point to things that can or cannot be changed? How do you sense that divine grace is guiding you?

Twelve-step groups keep participants accountable and offer guidance through sponsor relationships, but all of us need others who offer support with guidance as a secondary consideration. We do this to learn more in the way of truth, justice, and love. That gift of discernment undergirds and supports the whole of the first sentence of the Serenity Prayer.

The Unfamiliar Portion

Enter now the lesser-known part of the Serenity Prayer. The prayer moves more deeply into our spiritual hopes, and its connection with the power of God's divine love also grows. As we pray the latter portion of the prayer, we move toward a deeper acceptance of our lives and the gifts we have received. We also relinquish our efforts to control all outcomes. We do not give up power within ourselves or our goals and dreams, but we give up our fantasies of changing or controlling others.

Such a simple phrase is tucked in the Serenity Prayer: "Living one day at a time, enjoying one moment at a time." To live one day at a time and to enjoy one moment at a time seems an easy task, but we fail often in this undertaking. Our own minds work against us when it comes to living one day at a time and enjoying the present moment. Consider the work of the Ego. I think of the Ego in this very simplified way: the Ego serves to protect us when it feels the promise or threat of change. When that happens, Ego either projects an alternate vision of an ideal future in which all things are fulfilled allowing us to move to that ideal place in our thinking, or Ego takes us back to the past where we experienced a sort of safety. We can allow Ego to let us live safely in the past and not worry about coming change. One problem with such Ego devices is that we still cannot stop change from happening, and we fail to live in the present. Twelve-step participants understand this concept very well and remind one another to take one day at a time.

We also find ourselves playing the evasive game of "Someday"—"Someday when the children are grown, I'll ____" or "Someday when I pay off my debts, I'll ____." We can fill in the blanks with "go to Tahiti" or "visit Antarctica" or "finish that painting" or "learn to play the tuba." Another form of thinking that evades the present is "What if"—"What if I had listened to that teacher twenty years ago?" or "What if I had joined the Marine Corps?" or "What if my father had not died when I was six?" or "What if I hadn't made impulsive choices?". Either "Someday" or "What if" will take us far from enjoying the gifts of the moment. Live one day at a time and live, as William Saroyan wrote:

> so that in that good time there shall be no ugliness or death for yourself or for any life your life touches. Seek goodness every-where, and when it is found, bring it out of its hiding place and let it be free and unashamed. . . .
>
> In the time of your life, live—so that in that wondrous time you shall not add to the misery and sorrow of the world, but shall

smile to the infinite delight and mystery of it. (from *The Time of Your Life*)

From living one day at a time, the Serenity Prayer moves us into still deeper territory: "Accepting hardship as a pathway to peace." How can hardship become a path to peace? The phrase seems to go against the grain of what we believe or accept as true and right. We tend to think of peace as an absence of difficulty or struggle, and here Niebuhr offers what seems an opposite perspective. The phrase invites us to return to the opening of the prayer: "God, give me grace to accept with serenity . . . ." From that opening, we may begin to pray, "Give me grace to accept hardship as an ordinary part of life." Hardship is an everyday part of life. We are humans with limited time and limited talents and limited abilities. We experience the effects of an economic depression and feel sad that our friend the gifted teacher now works for less money on the loading dock of a warehouse and expresses gratitude for that job. We love, and too often those we love face crises that hurt them and hurt us. We watch our families and friends face disease or divorce or death, and we experience pain. We deal with the gifts and limitations of our genetic inheritance. We discover that we have a genetic predisposition toward a specific disease. We cannot accomplish all that we would like because time limits us. We do not have the capacity of infinite individual life on earth. We cannot control the world. We deal with other people and with bureaucracies and processes and procedures that are established by others. In short, as Scott Peck suggested in *The Road Less Traveled*, hardship happens. Once we accept that difficulties fill life, we begin to face reality in an honest way. Hardship happens and we invite God to keep us on a path toward peace rather than to allow hardship to keep us frozen in one psychic place for the rest of our lives. We ask God for the gift to accept hardship as we continue our life journey in peace to peace.

Niebuhr's prayer invites us to look at the person of Jesus, and I invite you to read the New Testament Gospel of Mark as a way to understand Jesus. The book is short. It does not contain the heavy emphasis of church found in the Gospels of Matthew and Luke, and it does not contain the philosophical and theological symbolism found in the Gospel of John. When you read the Gospel of Mark, you meet a Jesus who lives in the day, who deals immediately with the tasks at hand, and who accepts other people as they are. Mark presents a Jesus whose purpose is clear, and yet he willingly accommodates many who interrupt him because of their needs. Jesus accepts the world as it is: imperfect, flawed, and needy. He cares for those in need. He invites those around him to a deeper relationship with God. He reminds the people that the most important things are to love God and to love neighbor as one loves oneself.

Jesus does not project a sense of perfection upon the world. He does not exert control over others. He teaches, heals, exorcises, and feeds, and then he invites the recipients of these gifts to go in peace. Jesus prefers that they love one another and God, but he simply blesses and lets the people go.

Niebuhr understood that humanity is created in the image of God, and yet the world is a broken and sinful place. In *Moral Man and Immoral Society*, Niebuhr wrote: "The religious dimension of sin is . . . [the] effort to usurp the place of God. The moral and social dimension of sin is injustice. The ego which falsely makes itself the centre of existence in its pride and will-to-power inevitably subordinates other life to its will and thus does injustice to other life" (*The Nature and Destiny of Man*, vol. 1, p. 179). Niebuhr based his understanding on the twin conditions of human existence: finite time and free choice or free will. Given the limitations of time and the infinite possibility of choice, we struggle and our choices always have unintended consequences. Realize the obvious: every human being faces the limitations of time and the infinite possibility of choice. The choices made by every person flow throughout the world, contributing to the healing and the brokenness.

Jesus accepted the finite nature and the brokenness of the world. Jesus did not perform supernatural actions to reform the nature of humanity. He accepted, and we strive to accept: "taking this sinful world as it is, not as I would have the world." Every one of us envisions a perfect world and a perfect universe, formed according to our specifications and perhaps in our own image. Each fantasy world we create soon devolves as we clutch the fantasy in the midst of a reality that will not play along. Each fantasy world created for us—whether by marketing people or by game inventors or film makers—propels us further from a realistic perspective of the world. Far better to pray with Niebuhr that we receive the grace to accept with serenity the world as it is rather than the world that we project or is projected for us.

Move further into the prayer to the phrase about trusting that God will make all things right "if I surrender to Your will." During the plague years of the fourteenth century, Dame Julian lived as an anchoress in Norwich, England. An anchoress lived secluded within the church walls, usually in a cell or small room built on to a wall of the church. Dame Julian, a well-educated woman, gave spiritual guidance to those who sought her. She received visions from God and wrote about them. In her Thirteenth Revelation, Julian of Norwich wrote: "It behoved that there should be sin; but all shall be well, and all shall be well, and all manner of thing shall be well." Her perspective in the midst of the dreaded plague and death refreshes us still today. Despite the problems we face, we still believe that all shall be well in God's time. This sense of wellness or wholeness allows us to say yes, as Dag Hammarskjold did, to all that will come as we seek to give ourselves to the will of God. And what is the will of God? The biblical prophet Micah answers that question in this way: "to do justice, and to love kindness, and to walk humbly with your God" (Micah 6:8). As we seek to love kindness and to do justice for the greater good of all who live and the earth itself, so we offer ourselves to God. Without a sense of the divine love and kindness and justice, we would rely solely upon our projections and thus create a god in our own image.

Niebuhr closes the prayer in the same hope expressed by Julian of Norwich and many other Christian thinkers. Join the beginning and the end of this prayer: "Give me grace to accept . . . so that I may be reasonably happy in this life and supremely happy with You forever in the next." Lovett Weems and Tom Berlin, in a book titled *Bearing Fruit*, point out the importance of the words "so that" in many Bible verses. Their work addresses Christian congregations, and they rightly say that the conjunction "so that" points to purpose and mission. As we pray the full Serenity Prayer, we join in understanding a larger purpose of life. We pray for God's gift to be *reasonably* happy in the midst of the difficulty or hardship of existence, and for the supreme joy of an eternal life in the presence of God. Focus on the word that modifies happy. To be reasonably happy means that we accept ourselves as we are, not caught up in envy of those whose lives are different from our own nor trapped by the seductive efforts of commercial consumer culture. To pray with Niebuhr is to recognize that we have enough and that our faith is sufficient for the present moment. Firmly grounded in the present, the prayer does not project into that eternal future. It simply speaks to a hope, which we share across the various boundaries of nation and culture, of an eternal life of joy.

I invite you to begin praying the full version of the Serenity Prayer as an antidote to the tricks of Ego and temptations of culture for more and better. As you pray, remember what it implies about life in the present moment and the hope it offers for eternity. The Serenity Prayer reflects and embraces what we need as we face the ordinary reality of each day: mercy, mercy, mercy.

> God, give me grace to accept with serenity
> the things that cannot be changed,
> Courage to change the things
> which should be changed,
> and the Wisdom to distinguish
> the one from the other.
> Living one day at a time,
> Enjoying one moment at a time,
> Accepting hardship as a pathway to peace,
> Taking, as Jesus did,
> This sinful world as it is,
> Not as I would have it,
> Trusting that You will make all things right,

If I surrender to Your will,
So that I may be reasonably happy in this
   life,
And supremely happy with You forever in
   the next.
Amen.

Prayer

3

Orchestra:
The Rabbi's Prayer

If the two lines from Hammarskjold are a scale or an arpeggio, a musical exercise for the learning and practice of technique, and the Serenity Prayer is a group experience, then the Rabbi's Prayer is a symphony that calls for the blending of different voices in an orchestra and chorus. Here is one English-language version derived from the Gospel of Matthew:

Our Father who art in heaven,
hallowed be thy name
Thy kingdom come,
Thy will be done, on earth as in heaven.
Give us this day our daily bread.
And forgive us our trespasses,
As we forgive those who trespass against us.

And lead us not into temptation,
But deliver us from evil.
For thine is the kingdom,
and the power, and the glory,
for ever and ever. Amen.

Here is the transliterated Armenian version of that prayer:

Hayr Mer, vor hergines yes,
soorp yeghitsi anoon ko.
Yegestse arkayootyoon ko.
Yeghitsin gamk ko
vorbes hergines yev hergri.
Ez-hats mer hanabazort
dour mez aysor.
Yev togh mez ezbardis mer,
vorbes yev mek toghoomk merots bardabanats.
Yev mee danir uz mezee portsootyoon,
ayl pergya ee charen.
Zee ko eh arkayootyoon
yev zorootyoon
yev park havidyanes.
Amen.

Different words, same thoughts.

I have joined many other people in praying this prayer. I have prayed it in Roman Catholic congregations and in Lutheran ones, at Baptist funerals and independent services. I have prayed the prayer in Armenian and in English. I have sung the prayer to tunes written by classical composers and to tunes that came from folk traditions. In praying it, I have used the word "trespasses" in some settings and the word "debts" in the same phrase in other settings and the word "sins" in still other places. I have prayed the prayer silently. I have prayed this same prayer in ecumenical gatherings in which we were encouraged to pray in our native language or in our heart language. Our voices might have sounded like a cacophony to an uninformed observer; however, I believe that prayer spoken simultaneously in multiple languages offered insight into the prayer Jesus gave to unite his disciples. Just as the many different instruments in an orchestra sound different pitches each with a different quality to their tone and yet produce a cohesive sound, so the Lord's Prayer brings connection to a multitude of people of differing talents, gifts, cultures, and experiences. Given these multiple realities, I think of this prayer as a gift from Jesus for unity among all who seek God.

Because the prayer is familiar, perhaps we fail to understand or appreciate its depth. We think of this prayer as representing ancient tradition, which we may label as stale or meaningless; however, ancient tradition once was fresh and new and can be again. The prayer or its tradition is not the problem as much as the attitude with which we perceive the tradition.

If we expect a music festival to bore us, it will. If we expect any ceremony to bore us, we will experience boredom. If we anticipate an event with openness, we can receive the gifts of that event. Our best experiences happen when we live as Reinhold Niebuhr wrote in the Serenity Prayer, "one day at a time."

As an adolescent, I had friends who would go to Saturday confession before Roman Catholic mass. After they came out from confession, I would ask, "What happened?" As a curious non-Roman Catholic, I wanted to know about the practice.

"Oh, nothing bad. I told the priest that I had a case of lust. He told me to say three Hail Marys and ten Our Fathers as punishment."

The first time I heard this description of the aftermath of confession, I felt a little surprise. We went on with our Saturday night plans. After hearing my friend Steve repeat the same instruction for penance—*not punishment*—week after week, I began to roll my eyes and agree with him that the whole practice seemed archaic and superstitious. Roman Catholic teaching does not support our childish and adolescent understanding, and I do not want to contribute to misunderstanding or to prejudice concerning an abiding global community of faith. It never occurred to my adolescent thinking (or to my friend's thinking) that the priestly response to his confession was less about punishment or penance and far more about becoming open to God. Prayer is about opening ourselves to God's grace and love.

Consider what our misunderstanding of prayerful penitence implied about God. If prayer is understood as punishment, then what image of God supports such a perspective? God becomes the Great Gotcha in the Sky who waits for us to screw up in our daily living. Or God becomes a wrathful presence who must be appeased by saying certain words. Underlying these interpretations is the subtle argument that God is not as intelligent as we are: if God were as intelligent as we are, we would not fool God with our actions.

"Say a prayer and all will be OK." I wish life were that simple. My adolescent misunderstanding of the Catholic sacrament of penance and the television preacher's notion of placing a hand on the television screen and **"praying these words"** reveal magical thinking, but nothing that resembles a relationship with God. Magical thinking happens when we try to bargain with God about an exam or a work assignment for which we are not prepared or, more often, about an illness or a breaking relationship. We try to bargain with God, promising that we will change our lives if God will simply do as we demand. That kind of thinking takes us far from the reality of the prayers in this book, especially the prayer of Jesus. When we engage in magical thinking, we no longer live in the present moment nor do we take the world as it is. Instead of magical thinking, I hope that we can become open in our relationships with the divine reality.

The Rabbi Prays

According to sources, a rabbi was praying one day in a certain place. When he had finished praying, one of his followers came to him and said, "Lord, teach us to pray." In response to that request, rabbi Jesus offered his followers a simple prayer, which in English is about forty words. Another version of this prayer totals fifty-eight words. His prayer is recorded in the Gospel of Luke and the Gospel of Matthew. Luke's version (Luke 11:1–4) is the shorter version of the prayer (see Matthew 6:5–15). The context for teaching the prayer is also slightly different in these two books.

We do not usually identify Jesus of Nazareth as a rabbi. Without any effort on my part to prove anything about Jesus, for our conversation I invite you to take him at face value. Try to eliminate the layers of history—church history, political history, religious history—that have stuck to him. Try to eliminate the good and bad sermons or lectures you may have heard or that you may have tried not to hear. For that matter, try to eliminate the various artistic representations that cover a broad spectrum of tastes.

As I read the four Gospels, I see someone who invites others to learn and to do as he taught, a divine–human being, the essence of holiness in human form. Let's focus on the words of this prayer given by Jesus to his disciples.

When the disciples say to Jesus, "Teach us to pray," they invite a response from Jesus. In reality they are asking Jesus one of the most basic questions of spirituality. Their question is one I've asked in different ways: *How do I connect with God? How can I feel certain that God listens to prayer?* Then eventually comes my follow-up question: *How do I grow in my understanding and belief in God?* I think other questions are implied in that request from the unnamed disciple to Jesus. *What are the words appropriate to prayer? What assurance can I have that God hears my prayer? How would I know? How does God relate to humanity?* My questions may be your questions, and our questions reflect our spiritual condition.

Before we dig into the prayer, I invite you to consider its biblical context and to use your imagination to envision what is happening with the disciples and Jesus. The twelve disciples of that inner circle and others must have seen Jesus retreating from the crowds to be alone not once, but on a regular basis. Jesus simply goes away from the disciples. His time away may vary, but he returns to the disciples perhaps more refreshed than he had been before he left them. Imagine the conversation among the disciples, who are presented in the Gospels—especially the Gospel of Mark—as not understanding Jesus:

"Where does he go?"
"I don't know. He doesn't say."

"Where could he go? There's no place
   around here."
"Maybe he just goes away."
"Yes, I understand that, but where?"
"There's desert out there. He could go
   anywhere."
"There's desert around here. Why go away
   from us?"

Finally the disciples find courage to ask Jesus himself where he goes. "I go to be by myself and pray to the Creator." The disciples think that over, and then comes the request: "Teach us to pray." I imagine that Jesus responds with a smile because the disciples are beginning to understand something of his purpose and his relationship to God. So Jesus teaches a short prayer, one that probably was repeated many times during Jesus' public ministry. We may identify the prayer as a *kaddish*, a prayer taught and prayed by rabbis. Kaddish is recited on any number of occasions, such as Torah study or with mourners or at the end of a synagogue service. Kaddish may also signal a transition in worship. Maybe that sense of transition is what Jesus points toward in this prayer: God has promised and God is delivering; thanks be to God!

So you and I begin, like the disciples, with our question. How are we to understand prayer? How are we to practice prayer? We pray. We begin a daily practice in which we become open to God's love. We offer our breath prayers and we let the prayers of

Dag Hammarskjold, Reinhold Niebuhr, and Jesus of Nazareth become part of our inner lives.

The Prayer

I invite you to look at the whole of the prayer and to pray it in its entirety. Whether you regularly attend worship or feel a deep spirituality, but are not particularly committed to any institution, we know this prayer and know a little about the tradition. We memorize it, perhaps not intentionally, but simply because of having heard others pray the prayer so frequently. Our own familiarity with the prayer shades our understanding. We know the phrases and we can say them without thinking, but that rote expression may also mean that we are not paying attention to what comes from our lips. The next time you pray this prayer, take time to contemplate the individual phrases because each phrase offers its own depth of meaning.

To pray the whole prayer, we might begin with an exercise in deconstruction and take the prayer apart. We could look at different words and phrases, unpack their meaning, examine the biblical roots of these words, mentally caress these words, and then begin to reconstruct the prayer. Many authors explore the various phrases of this prayer, and these authors bring their own perspectives to their study. Author X brings passionate wisdom to the prayer. Author Y focuses on piety and spirituality. Another author may examine the prayer's ethical foundation. Another author enables us to see the all-encompassing nature of the prayer. I invite you to find yourself and your longings in this prayer. To do that, I want to look at three portions of Jesus' prayer:

> Thy kingdom come, thy will be done
>   on earth as in heaven.
> Give us this day our daily bread.
> Forgive us our trespasses, as we forgive those
>   who trespass against us.

Earth and Heaven

"Thy kingdom come, thy will be done on earth as in heaven" is a relatively long clause in the prayer and one that seems easy to overlook because the petition appears otherworldly in its intent. I need to set aside my jaundiced perspective on monarchy whenever I think about God's kingdom. I do not much care for the ways of royalty on earth. Neither am I an admirer of the so-called royal families. History shows us the many failures of monarchs in dealing with the human beings surrounding them. Think of Herod the Great, king of Judea from 30 BCE until 4 BCE. Herod executed his first wife, his brother-in-law, his sons. He plotted against others he perceived as rivals. Noting Torah declared pork unclean, Augustus Caesar quipped that he would rather be Herod's pig than Herod's son. Herod the Great is one of many examples of royalty gone wild. Royal families have oppressed and enslaved people, ruined nations (others and their own) while seeking power, and they have indiscriminately destroyed people and creation. Why should biology give power to those who are little concerned for others who live within the boundaries of their territory? Why should disinterested royalty receive rewards? I do know that some monarchs have been just and good leaders. I also know that the history of representative governments and legislative bodies contains many stories of corruption and indecency. Earthly governments honor and give more power to those who already have power or who conform to the system. The practical values demonstrated by such governments grow from the pursuit of further power. Governments attempt to gain more power and influence over other nations. They may try to consolidate power. One group of politicians may attempt to build a coalition of power, which then replicates the actions of those who were replaced. The new boss acts the same as the old boss! A biblical understanding of the kingdom or reign of God is different from all these maneuvers. So let's think of God's kingdom as something quite opposite from the way that governments function on earth.

To think about the reign or kingdom of God invites us to look at the first portion of the Bible. The writer of Genesis shows us a universe that is orderly and at peace. Birds, animals, plants, and humans are together in an orderly creation described as a garden. Looking back at that primordial history, we see an innocent world, a world in which Genesis says, "to every beast of the earth, and to every bird of the air, and to everything that creeps on the earth, everything that has the breath of life, I have given every green plant for food" (Genesis 1:30). This peaceful vision includes no need to kill even for food while living in this garden.

As I consider the story of creation and the Lord's Prayer, I wonder about that kingdom or reign of God. What if that initial vision of life is God's vision for the world? What if God wants us to move from our state of broken and wounded humanity toward a future garden in which all creation lives again in a harmonious convergence of love and justice? Such a vision brings to my mind the grandeur and glory of Beethoven's Ninth Symphony!

Jesus refers to the kingdom of God in many parables and sayings. What does he mean when he speaks of the kingdom? While there is much debate concerning what Jesus meant, let's look at some facets of the kingdom of God that may have been part of Jesus' understanding. These characteristics of the kingdom grow from the Law and Prophets and Writings of Judaism. The writers of the psalms and the prophets speak of God's reign as one of justice.

While working on another project, I asked people to tell me their understanding of justice. Their responses all focused on the court system, at best a mixed bag of justice and injustice. The current system, more specifically known as retributive justice, seems only to seek ways to populate jails and prisons. Retributive justice is the legal understanding of justice that goes back in time to the Code of Hammurabi around the year 1772 BCE. We may summarize Hammurabi's Code by referring to "an eye for an eye." Retributive justice seeks to redress crime and loss with proportionate punishment. Contrast retributive justice with restorative justice. Restorative justice seeks reconciliation. Restorative justice focuses on the needs of victims and offenders. The Truth and Reconciliation Commission in South Africa practiced restorative justice after the end of apartheid, allowing victims to testify to the ways in which they were harmed and offenders to hear the testimony and seek resolution. Restorative justice takes more personal investment than retributive justice. Restorative justice relies less on legal principles and trickery and far more on the basic interaction of human with human. Restorative justice aims to create communities of respect and peace for all life. To me, that is the way of God's justice and God's kingdom.

One of the more poignant prophetic passages is the allegory in Isaiah 5. Here Isaiah speaks for God about a vineyard. Planted with care, the vineyard has the best grapes and the best conditions for growth.

My beloved had a vineyard on a very fertile
hill.

He dug it and cleared it of stones,
　　and planted it with choice vines . . .
he expected it to yield grapes,
　　but it yielded wild grapes.
And now, inhabitants of Jerusalem . . .
What more was there to do for my vineyard
　　that I have not done in it? . . .
I will remove its hedge,
　　and it shall be devoured.
I will break down its wall,
　　and it shall be trampled down.
I will make it a waste. (Isaiah 5:1–6)

Those to whom the vineyard was entrusted neglected
it. We move from the promised beauty of the vineyard to something that stands in ruins. The creator of
the vineyard responds in anger. The prophet explains
the basis for that anger:

He expected justice,
　　but saw bloodshed;
righteousness,
　　but heard a cry! (Isaiah 5:7)

Isaiah then denounces the people and describes their
social injustices. These injustices include greed and
hoarding land. Within the Hebrew Bible are many
commandments concerning the nature of community and the common good. Our twenty-first century Western perspective causes us to read these

commandments as rules for individuals; however, the collective concern of the biblical commandments is for the holiness of the nation. The greed of an individual, for example, in taking the property that rightfully belonged to a widow wronged the surviving spouse and many others because such greed damaged the holiness of the community. Rather than steal from a widow, the biblical command is to care for widows and orphans. We see a prime example in the Book of Ruth when Boaz, a property owner, leaves grains in the field for gleaning and finds other ways to care for Ruth the widow. The apostle Paul builds upon this understanding in addressing the Corinthian church: "If one member suffers, all suffer together" (1 Cor. 12:26). The biblical perspective concerns the ways in which all individuals are connected with one another. In other passages, Isaiah complains about the nation's injustice in cheating widows and stealing from orphans. In the first chapter of Isaiah are these words of instruction:

> Cease to do evil,
> learn to do good;
> seek justice,
> rescue the oppressed,
> defend the orphan,
> plead for the widow. (Isaiah 1:16–17)

In God's kingdom, widows and orphans will receive protection; predators will not cheat widows and orphans. Their land and other goods will not be stolen, and those who have power will not trample the rights of the powerless. In God's kingdom the hungry will have plenty of food and plenty to drink. Sojourners and aliens will receive welcome hospitality. In this reign of God, healing will happen. In the reign of God, prisoners will be set free and will live in peace with former adversaries. Justice and mercy will embrace, and love and compassion will walk together with justice and mercy. *Thy kingdom come* becomes a plea for justice and a call to act for the sake of God's justice and mercy.

Whenever we pray these words, we invite God's radical actions for justice and we commit ourselves to strive for that same justice that is the kingdom of God. The coming of God's reign is a foundation for all of Jesus' teachings and he spoke often of this kingdom.

The petition does not end with "Thy kingdom come," but continues with "Thy will be done." Many people get hung up as they try to understand God's will for their lives. They dither and deal with an inner puzzle in the hope that they will discover what God wants them to do in each moment and each decision of their lives. They ponder whether their actions are God's will. In the way that they wrangle the question, the answer is simple: God does not care about work or spouse or house or any of our many specific and concrete questions. However, that does not mean that God does not care for us or that we cannot know

God's will. The will of God matters. The will of God is justice and mercy and love. The will of God mirrors the kingdom of God. Recall that the kingdom of God comes in justice and mercy, compassion and love. The will of God also exercises those same qualities. Do the questions about work or spouse or house also concern justice and mercy and love? Will justice and mercy and love be made manifest in choices of work or spouse or house? If so, then that is God's will for you.

To pray that God's will be done is to pray that widows and orphans receive care, that aliens, refugees, sojourners, and those without appropriate documentation receive hospitality. God's will can turn our usual ways of being in the world upside down because God values things according to those life-giving qualities of justice, mercy, and compassion.

These three phrases go together: "Thy kingdom come / thy will be done / on earth as in heaven." But before putting them together, play with the words so that the phrase reads, "thy will be done in heaven as on earth." What a horrible image if the will of God were done in heaven as it is now on earth! If the will of God is done in heaven as on earth, the heavenly beings are arguing, fighting, protecting turf, and trying to claim more. Suddenly the many beautifully peaceful images of heaven morph into yet another place where haves and have-nots are at odds. The scene becomes a nightmare, a bizarre vision that may jolt us to think differently about this portion of the Lord's Prayer. Leave those images of heaven-become-imperfect-earth behind. Reflect instead on this prayer:

> May thy will be done on earth
> as it is done in heaven.

Jesus' phrase reflects a great hope that we will be made perfect in love in this life so that through our lives others see the gifts of God's love. When we pray this prayer by rote, we may not consider the nuances of meaning that are packed within those seven simple words: "Thy kingdom come, thy will be done." Pray these words without the words that precede or follow them. Contemplate the words. What does God say to you about the kingdom? How do you understand the will of God on earth as in heaven?

Daily Bread

"Give us this day our daily bread." I have heard teachers and preachers say that this prayer concerns all of our needs and that it reminds us to depend on God for all things. Did Jesus mean that we rely on God for all our physical needs or did he intend basic food? Consider that in other places Jesus spoke quite specifically about relying on God's grace to clothe and feed us and care for our needs. In the Sermon on the Mount (Matthew 6:25–34), Jesus specified clothing, food, and other physical needs, and taught that God knew that we needed these things; however, he ends this section by saying, "Strive first for the kingdom of God . . . and all these things will be given to you as well." I think that within this prayer, Jesus really means basic food with an implicit reminder that we are grateful to God for this sustenance.

Our attitude and understanding of this portion of the prayer grows from our economic situation. If we live in relative affluence, we may jump over this petition. If we live beneath the poverty lines, this petition may be our heart's deepest cry or lament. If we recognize that people throughout history and throughout many different nations join in this prayer, then the prayer for daily bread becomes a cry for justice. Christians who live in zones of famine pray the same words as do Christians who live in areas of plenty.

I don't normally worry about my food needs. I've traveled and eaten in some unusual settings. For a short period I dined daily at Christ Church College of Oxford University, the dining hall seen in the Harry Potter films. I've dined in a restaurant on the side of a mountain in Armenia where the fish came directly from the mountain stream. I've also dined with families in Appalachia and in the poorest of shacks in South Africa where I experienced the gracious hospitality of deep poverty. The people provided food that they had grown or that had been given to them by neighbors to honor their guest. I felt uneasy eating food that was much more than their usual fare. I also knew that I did not want to insult anyone by refusing to eat. Give us this day our daily bread.

What happens when we connect Jesus' words about the coming of God's kingdom with "Give us this day our daily bread"? What if we let go of our anxieties and fears about the future and let today's possibilities be enough? We stop hoarding food and other possessions for the future. We begin to share our resources with those who have less. What if Jesus expects us to share our gifts with others? What if Jesus expects us to give without attaching proofs and conditions? On several occasions Jesus took small amounts of bread and fish, gave thanks to God for these gifts, and then fed thousands of people with those meager resources. He did not question the needs of any of the 5,000 people fed with the five loaves of bread and two fish (Mark 6:30–44). Nor did Jesus give eligibility tests to the 4,000 people fed with seven loaves and "a few small fish" (Mark 8:1–10). He simply fed people. In the Gospel of Matthew, Jesus surprises people by inviting them to "inherit the kingdom prepared for you . . . for I was hungry and you gave me food" (Matthew 25:34–35). There comes the startled response of those welcomed by Jesus: "When did we feed you?" Jesus continues, "Just as you did it to one of the least of these who are members of my family, you did it to me" (see Matthew 25:31–46).

Global hunger is a complicated issue that goes beyond the scope of a book on prayer; it involves both food scarcity and the distribution of food, and it encompasses a variety of networks that include agri-business, financiers, farmers, brokers, and others. Denis van Waerebeke directed a short animated film, titled *How to Feed the World*, which offers some guidance.[2]

No matter the cause of hunger, whenever we pray, "Give us this day our daily bread," we also agree to act in the name of Jesus—to share what we have with those who do not have. God wants us to share our gifts— our bread—with one another and especially with those who have less than we have. When we pray these words about daily bread, we also pray for the reign of God's justice and peace. It is as simple as the kindergarten child sharing a jelly sandwich with another child who has no lunch. We need not put layers of qualification on our sharing. We need only open our eyes to the needs of the world—to the hunger of the world. Knowing that God cares for us, we are free to care for others.

Give us this day our daily bread. Care for our needs, we pray. Care for our needs and for the needs of those with whom we share life. Our prayer is one of gratitude and intercession.

The Matter of Forgiveness

Jesus said, "Forgive us our trespasses, as we forgive those who trespass against us." When we were

---

2 See the video at http://vimeo.com/8812686; accessed June 23, 2014.

adolescents, we equated trespasses with sins. One of my friends would say, "I'm a Baptist. I don't smoke, drink, cuss, or think." Then he would inhale his cigarette or swallow some beer and smile. All the group would laugh at this expression of hip cynicism. We understood that the Baptists in our area branded those four actions as sins.

An adult friend said, "I don't understand why I need to offer any kind of prayer of confession because those prayers usually make a promise that I'll do better next time and I'm living about as good as I'm going to get. I don't cheat or lie or steal. I don't sin on purpose. I don't understand that 'forgive us our trespasses' business. Seems like empty words that get tossed around."

The word *sin* brings heavy baggage. Many people understand sin within a narrow moralistic view of behavior; if we do not cross certain lines, then all is right with us. We imagine some supreme accountant who places our thoughts and actions on either the credit or debit side of the cosmic ledger. To think of sin as behaviors on a morality spreadsheet of good and evil underestimates our imperfect human nature. When Jesus finished teaching this prayer to those who followed him, he concluded: "For if you forgive others their trespasses, your heavenly Father will also forgive you; but if you do not forgive others, neither will your Father forgive your trespasses" (Matthew 6:14–15).

An aside: I think that we are capable of missing a much larger reality when we rush to condemn the sins of others: All people, fragile and limited as we are, live in the grace of God, and God extends that grace, known also as unconditional love, to all people. Instead of angry shouting matches in which Bible verses are hurled like thunderbolts and lightning from Valhalla, our conversation should begin to look at the nature of sin as not loving what God loves—and God loves all. Sin is not caring for the needy and the hungry, not visiting the sick and bringing healing to them, not visiting those in prison and offering freedom. Sin replaces the way of peace with the escalating development of weapons of destruction. These ways go against the will of God and the coming reign of God. Sin is not simply a matter of being human.

When we label others and identify their sins or cast blame, we fail to look within ourselves. Jesus elsewhere offered a statement about sin that serves as moral guidance:

> Do not judge, so that you may not be
>   judged.
> For with the judgment you make you will
>   be judged,
> and the measure you give will be the
>   measure you get.
> Why do you see the speck in your neighbor's
>   eye,

but do not notice the log in your own eye?
(Matthew 7:1–3)

One of the difficulties in a conversation about sin
happens when someone says, "I'm about as good as
I'm going to get, but those others . . . ." What we
fail to notice when we make such a statement is our
own pride, which the ancient Greeks called *hubris*.
Such pride goes against the divine law that speaks
of loving our neighbor as ourselves. Arrogance
does not love; rather, arrogance looks down upon
others. When we cast ourselves as better than others
because "we're about as good as possible," then we
are committing the sin of pride, which is no less and
no more than any other sin. I dined with a group
who had been leaders on the Walk to Emmaus, an
intensive three-day course in Christian disciple-
ship. In conversation with the man sitting opposite
me, I learned that he worked as a vice-president of a
financial institution and spent time working in the
Kairos ministry, a version of the Emmaus experience set in prisons. I asked, "What have you learned
from going into the prisons?" "I learned that the
only difference between many of those behind bars
and me is that I've had the good fortune to not be
caught. I've changed my attitude about myself and
about those in the prison system. I realize that we
are very much brothers and sisters in Christ." That
night I learned another lesson about the folly of
stereotyping.

Trespass helps us to see something different from sin. Trespass refers to an unlawful act that causes injury or harm to the person, property, or rights of another person, whether that action was committed with violence and was actual or implied. When Jesus speaks of forgiveness for trespasses, he brings us again to the need for reconciliation among all people and a restoration to the values of God's kingdom.

"Forgive us our trespasses, as we forgive those who trespass against us," Jesus said, and "Do not judge, so that you may not be judged" (Matthew 7:1). Jesus is clear on this need for forgiveness, which begins with our awareness of our own failures and short-comings, our actions and our inactions. Forgiveness may not seem easy, but it remains the healthy and right action. We forgive and we let go. Some injuries remain on the surface and are gone as quickly as they arrived. Other wounds go deep and will not be healed in a moment or a day, but will need time and focus for release.[3] We practice forgiving others and we practice forgiving ourselves. As we forgive ourselves and forgive others, we also seek divine guidance and guidance from those we trust to better the ways in which we act in the world. To forgive means

---

3 Flora Slosson Wuellner addresses wounds and healing in a number of her books, especially *Release: Healing from Wounds of Family, Church, and Community; Prayer, Stress, and Our Inner Wounds;* and *Forgiveness: the Passionate Journey.* Wuellner writes about these wounds and offers guided prayer meditations that bring the healing love of God to these places of hurt.

that we grow in love for others, for the earth, and for all that God creates.

To forgive those who trespass against us brings us back to the symphonic nature of this prayer: Jesus invites his followers to seek the values that embody God's reign, in our various voices and contexts. To pray that God's kingdom come on earth is to seek God's will for ourselves and for all creation. God's will values love and justice, mercy and compassion. As we act with mercy and compassion toward others and ourselves, we become much more like Jesus. We become people who embody justice, mercy, and love for all people and all creation.

AFTERWORD OR MUSICAL STING

A stinger (or musical sting) is usually an ending that serves to punctuate the composition. Think of the antique musical phrase: "Shave and a haircut—two bits" (dah-da-da-dah-da—Pum-Pum). The last two notes are the sting. The last two notes (or syllables) provide an exclamation point. Why am I writing this? I am trying to write one final note about these prayers, but I may have written enough already. Still I want to offer a last note.

Throughout the writing of this book, I have prayed the three prayers plus a variety of breath prayers. Here are the three prayers in one place.

The Diplomat Hammarskjold:

> For all that has been—Thanks!
> To all that shall be—Yes!

The Theologian Niebuhr:

> God, give me grace to accept with serenity
> the things that cannot be changed,
> Courage to change the things
> which should be changed,

and the Wisdom to distinguish
the one from the other.
Living one day at a time,
Enjoying one moment at a time,
Accepting hardship as a pathway to peace,
Taking, as Jesus did,
This sinful world as it is,
Not as I would have it,
Trusting that You will make all things right,
If I surrender to Your will,
So that I may be reasonably happy in
    this life,
And supremely happy with You forever
    in the next.
Amen.

The Rabbi Jesus:

Our Father in heaven,
    hallowed be your name,
    your kingdom come,
    your will be done on earth as in heaven.
Give us today our daily bread.
Forgive us our sins
    as we forgive those who sin against us.
Save us from the time of trial
    and deliver us from evil.
For the kingdom, the power, and the glory
    are yours
    now and for ever. Amen.

I offer an ecumenical version of this last prayer. The Rabbi's Prayer comes in many versions and translations. Every language reflects the wealthy nuances of a particular culture. In Armenian, for example, we begin by praying *Hayr Mer*, literally Father Our, but that is a peculiarity of Armenian syntax. No matter the language or form, this prayer seems a foundation for our deepening and ongoing relationship with God. You may know by memory or by heart another version of the prayer.

I invite you to pray these prayers and to pray them on a routine and regular basis. Listen. Here is a pattern for daily practice of prayer: Begin the day with Hammarskjold's prayer. During the day—perhaps during a break or at lunch—pray Niebuhr's prayer. Close the day with the prayer of Jesus. Offer speech and silence to God.

An ancient joke: "How do I get to Carnegie Hall?" asked the man carrying an oboe case, walking out of the subway. Said the jaded New Yorker: "Practice." I invite you to lifelong practice.

ACKNOWLEDGMENTS

Writing a book, like much prayer, is primarily a solitary act, but both writing and prayer recall to memory a community of friends: those who are with us in the present and those who were with us in the past. Armenians like to gather things in threes, toast in threes, and bless in threes. Here I offer three sets of three.

I honor the memory of the three women who first taught me to pray: my biological mother Lucy Kamajian Donigian, my godmother Mariam Der Krikorian Minasian, and my neighborhood mother Mary Bobb Blaho.

I give thanks for three musicians who taught me how to read outside the lines and to realize through them that prayer always moves beyond words: Cannonball Adderley, Dave Brubeck, and John Coltrane.

I offer gratitude for the memory of three altogether different pastors who influenced my practice of prayer many years ago. They represent distinctly different traditions that influence me for better and worse: the Rev. Frank G. Koehler, pastor of Nazareth Lutheran Church (Missouri Synod), Hopewell,

Virginia; Col. George C. Patterson (USAF retired), Southern Baptist chaplain at Fork Union Military Academy; and the Rev. Larry A. Green, United Methodist chaplain at Berry College.

That Armenian tradition of toasting and acknowledging in threes can become a constraint. I offer thanksgiving also for the musical life of Komitas Vartabet, Armenian priest-musician and victim of genocide, whose biography and music taught me that we pray across borders and cultures even in those times when we do not understand the language of others.

And in my own explosive penultimate paragraph-and-last-chance-to-say-all-that-needs-saying way, here are nine other friends to whom I am grateful for many conversations about our common life: Steve Harper, K. Cherie Jones, and Roland Rink—co-workers at The Upper Room in the U.S. and South Africa, and Ann V. Butterworth, Steve Doughty, Safiyah Fosua, Kwasi Kena, Kathleen Stephens, and the Rhino.

For the publishing partnership with Nancy Bryan and Church Publishing Incorporated, I am grateful.